WHY ARE THEY
GHOSTING ME?

9 Reasons Why They're Not Replying
To Your Emails and Messages – and how to fix them

ALAN BERG, CSP
GLOBAL SPEAKING FELLOW

To my favourite –
whiskey-
drinking
buddy,

Love,
RC

Why Are They Ghosting Me? Wedding & Event Pro Edition
9 Reasons Why They're Not Replying To Your Emails and Messages
– and how to fix them

Paperback ISBN: 9798455577079

Published by:
Wedding Business Solutions, LLC &
Left of Center Marketing & Publishing
Kendall Park, NJ © 2021

Acknowledgements:
Editor: Carole Berg
Interior Book Design: Amit Dey & Ian Berg
Cover Design: Ian Berg

DEDICATION

This book is dedicated to Carole, the love of my life
and my best friend.

Despite having to listen to me for all these years, you
still help me edit my books and listen to my podcasts.
If that ain't love... ♥

TABLE OF CONTENTS

Preface – What is Ghosting?

If you're reading this, you're most likely a Wedding and/or Event professional. You either own, run or work at a venue, catering company or bridal shop; or maybe you're a DJ, photographer, band, florist, planner, officiant, or any of the other professionals that make weddings and events great. If you're not a wedding/event pro, or you also work outside the industry, the tips in this book can help you, too. Whether you work inside and/or outside the wedding/events industry, you've likely experienced getting an inquiry, replying as quickly as you can and then... nothing! No reply at all. Sound familiar? That's Ghosting! It should just be called "frustrating" because that's what it is. You think you did everything you were supposed to, the way you should, so why aren't they replying to you?

This book is the sequel to my book: *"Why Don't They Call Me? 8 tips for converting wedding and event inquiries into sales."* I chose that title because it's a phrase I hear over and over from frustrated wedding and event pros, like you. Many of you express to me that it would be so much easier for you if they would call or agree to get on a call with you. Whether you've been in the industry for 20 years or 20 days, it certainly would be easier...*for you!* However, if it were easier for your couples and clients... they would have called you. I joke that I almost made that the shortest book ever. The cover would say: "Why don't they call me?" and then inside it would simply say "Get over it!"

Whether you've read "Why Don't They Call Me?" or not, this book will help you reduce the ghosting. Yes, I said 'reduce' the ghosting, not eliminate it. I wish I could tell you that following the tips in this book will get everyone to reply to you, but I can't. Some things are just beyond our control. That said, clients of mine, and people who've heard me speak on this subject who are following these tips, are reporting to me that they're getting way more replies, having more good conversations, and making more sales. I'll summarize the 8 tips from "Why Don't They Call Me?" in a later chapter. For those of you who've read that book, it will be a good refresher. For those of you that have not read that book, it will give some context to the concepts in this book.

When you're the customer, you get to decide which method of communication is best for you. Sometimes you call. Other times you fill out a contact form or send an email. Maybe texting or WhatsApp is better for you. Sometimes a live chatting app on the company's website is your preference. Or maybe you decide to drive over and walk in to the office or store for that business. The key is that you're driving the communication process with the method you choose to start the conversation.

Have you ever wanted to call a company but there was no phone number on their site? I think we've all been there. How frustrating is that for you? When a company tries to move you to a communication method that's not convenient for you, or not your preference, they're adding friction to the customer experience. In his book: *"The Convenience Revolution"*, my good friend Shep Hyken (one of the leading customer service experts in the world) explains how companies can, and should, reduce the friction and make it easier for their customers. Whether it's the communication method(s), hours of availability or even how you present your services/packages, any friction in the process is a reason for a customer to look elsewhere. In this book I'll help you see the friction points in your process, so you can make it easier for your couples and clients to do business with you.

By the time you get an inquiry, that couple or customer has already put you on a short list of possible prospects. They are telegraphing to you that they already need what you do. You need to help them see that they need to get those products/services from *you*. I'll be talking more about how to do that later in this book. You'll see how to understand your 'why' and not just 'what' you do. You'll see how to express more about what makes you unique.

Before a couple or customer makes an inquiry, they've already done some research. They've seen that there are way too many choices for them, so they need to filter those choices down to a manageable few. In his book: *"The Paradox of Choice"*, Barry Schwartz talks about 'decision-paralysis.' That's when you have so many choices that you can't decide at all. Or you decide *not* to decide right now. Your job is to *reduce* their choices, not overwhelm them with more options. You can have many choices for them, but they can't all be right for their wedding, corporate event, mitzvah or other event. You should be eliminating the things that aren't right for them *before* you present them with possible solutions. You should not be showing everyone everything you can do.

One of my clients, a wedding/event venue, used to send every inquiry their menus on their first reply. It had menus for breakfast, brunch, lunch, buffet dinner, plated dinner, desserts, beverages and more. It was 40 pages! No one needs to see all of that. And if you know that they're planning an evening wedding, why would you send them breakfast, brunch, lunch, etc.? If you don't know what they're planning, why would you dump all of that data on them from the get-go?

As you work through the tips in this book, remember what it's like to be on the receiving end, as a customer. Doing what's easier for you, the business, often feels very different to the customer. Following the tips in this book can help you reduce the ghosting by wedding, social and corporate clients. It has worked for the many, many wedding and event pros, around the world, who've either heard me speak about this, or have had me do individual or group sales training. Thanks for taking this journey with me. You're on your way to having more and better conversations with your couples and clients. Those better conversations should lead to better conversion and sales. I hope you'll share your success stories with me.

The Opportunity Cost of Ghosting

When you get an inquiry, whether through your website, a direct email/text or through an online platform such as The Knot, WeddingWire, weddingsonline, EasyWeddings, Guides for Brides or through a social media channel, there are three possible outcomes:

1. You get a YES and get the sale!
2. You get a NO, they choose someone else - *or* -
3. You get Ghosted – no reply at all, or you get a reply, respond back and then get ghosted.

Which of those is the worst outcome? Many of you are thinking it's #2, hearing that they've booked someone else. I actually think it's #3, getting ghosted. Why? Because they already filtered all of the possible choices for your service/product down to a very short list, and you were on it. Most of your competitors don't even know that this couple or customer is looking for what you do. It's very likely that they're going to book someone for your service/product, as opposed to not getting it at all. Even if they decide to go with a 'friendor' (a friend or relative to do your product/service), you're getting closure on that lead.

"Opportunity cost" is defined as "the loss of potential gain from other alternatives when one alternative is chosen." [credit to Oxford Languages for the definition]. I define it more simply as the money you could have made but didn't! Someone is going to get that sale, why not you? And since you're getting ghosted, you don't know who they've booked, or if they've made a decision yet at all. And that's where the opportunity lies.

If you get ten new inquiries, and you get a resolution on four of them, a Yes or a No, what happened to the other six? How many of those still need your product/service? You don't know. If even one of those six ended up booking you, how much more profit would that mean to you? How many inquiries do you get in a week, a month or a year? If you could book one more for every ten you get, how much more business is that? How much more profit is that? For the wedding and event pros I've worked with, even a small increase can amount to hundreds, thousands, tens of thousands dollars or more in profits.

When you get a lead, I want you to be like a dog that's just been given a bone to chew on. No matter how nice the dog is, if you try to take that bone away the dog is going to want to keep it and finish chewing. You need to work that lead until it's finished, meaning that you got an answer, yes or no. Is it likely that you'll be able to get a resolution on every lead? Unfortunately, no. And I understand that it's frustrating as it happens to me, as well. But following the tips in this book will get you more resolutions than you did before, and some of those ghosts will turn into sales! You just have to accept that it's up to you to work those leads. This applies to wedding leads, quinceañera leads, non-profit event leads, corporate leads... yes, all leads.

The customers have already done their part. As a matter of fact, they started the process by making their inquiry. Whatever it is that they've already seen, heard, read, watched or experienced, has lead them to wanting to make an inquiry with you. It's so much easier to work a lead you've already gotten better than to try to get another new inquiry. You've just been handed the bone... don't let go until you're finished with it!

NOTES

THE FOUR STEPS TO MORE SALES

I do a lot of sales training, sometimes for an individual and other times for sales teams (large and small). My sales training brand is: "Your Personal Sales Trainer", because most wedding and event businesses can't afford, or justify having a full-time sales trainer on staff. We go through what I call "The Sales Circuit", which is the four steps to more sales:

1. Attract their attention
2. Get the inquiry
3. Have a conversation
4. Make the sale

Attracting their attention is key, because if you don't have their attention, they don't know you exist and therefore you're not even a choice for them to consider. You get their attention through advertising, marketing, networking, SEO (search engine optimization), referrals, social media and more. You want to be everywhere your prospective customers are when they're looking for your product or service for their wedding or event. Some of that requires an investment in time, some an investment in money and many require both. How and where to advertise is not the subject of this book, but I have spoken about it on my podcast (the Wedding Business Solutions Podcast) and some webinars. Advertising isn't about buying ads or taking booths at wedding expos and trade shows. It's about buying access to those audiences. The short answer is that you should invest in your business the way you want your couples and customers to invest in you. If you're looking for every free way to promote yourself, don't be surprised when you don't reach the right customers with the right budgets for your products/services.

After you get their attention, you need to tell them what to do next. You do this with calls-to-action. Just listing your web address or contact info isn't being specific, it's being ambiguous. I have little postcards I give to my clients that say: "Ambiguous Next Steps Bring Ambiguous Results." You need to tell them what to do and then make it easy to do it. That goes back to reducing the friction that I mentioned in the Preface. Don't just say: "Contact Us". Tell them why they should contact you and how. Try something like:

"To check our availability, get a price quote or arrange a meeting (phone or in-person), call, text, email or click here to contact us."

And you'd make it so the word "call" can be clicked to dial you. The word "text" would open a new text message when it's clicked, etc.

Tweak the wording of the call-to-action to be in context to what you were just speaking about in that ad, or on your website or social page. For example, if you're a wedding floral decorator, you could say:

"To find out just how beautiful your wedding flowers can be, call, text, email or contact us today."

The more specific you can be about what you're asking them to do, and more importantly, why it's important to them, the more people will do it. Using action buttons is a really good idea since so much of your website's traffic is coming through mobile devices. Just be specific on the button text as well. Saying: "Learn More" or "Read More" is ambiguous. Learn more about what? Read more about what?

Avoid high-commitment wording on your buttons and calls-to-action. Saying: "Book Us Now!" is a very high commitment. If someone just wants to ask a question, arrange a meeting or get a price quote, they're not going to want to click a button that says: "Book Us Now!" If you only have buttons that say: "Check Availability" or "Schedule an Appointment", you might also miss out on those that aren't ready for those, yet. And yes, I know that's what *you* want them to do. As I've said earlier, you have to think like a customer. You can give them those options alongside calling, emailing, texting, etc. Just don't make those the only options or you're adding some of that friction to the process.

I was doing a ghosting workshop and one of the participants' website only had the option of calling or texting. While I applaud him for the texting option, as so many couples are using that format, by not having an email option or contact form he's missing out on inquiries. I asked why he didn't have email or a contact form, and he said it was because he was getting too much spam. I told him that he's making it harder for the real prospects because he doesn't want to get the spam. That's punishing the real customers because of the spammers. He should be looking for a better spam filter rather than removing the email and contact form from his site. I have no doubt that he's lost business by not having an email or contact form option for his real prospects.

Once you've gotten their attention and they've made the inquiry, the conversation has been started... by the couple or customer. You're not trying to start a conversation, it's already been started. You want to move it forward. That's where this book comes in. I want you to get some tools that will help you continue the conversations that your couples and customers are starting with you, every time they make an inquiry. If they called, you would answer the phone or return their call. You'd continue the conversation with them, even though you don't know anything about them yet. You'll also see how some of the things that you're doing now are actually causing the ghosting. The computer geeks have a phrase for that. They say that the problem lies between the keyboard and the chair! I know that I suffer from that sometimes as well. It's in recognizing that the problem often lies with the person in the mirror, and that helps you make the necessary changes. After you continue the conversation, then you get to move forward towards the sale. Some of that is certainly in this book. For more specific wording on closing the sale you might want to read: "Shut Up and Sell More Weddings & Events" (if you haven't already).

Recap of Why Don't They Call Me?

In "Why Don't They Call Me?" I outline the 8 tips for converting wedding and event inquiries into sales. If you've read that book, this chapter will be a refresher (or feel free to skip ahead). If you've not read it yet, then this will give some context to some of the concepts in this book. Here are the 8 tips:

1. **It's a real conversation** – I know that sounds obvious, but so many people have a hard time writing the way they speak. When we do secret shopping (making inquiries with wedding and event pros as if we were real social or corporate prospects) we find a lot of rigid and formal sounding wording in your replies. Every person and every business has a voice. People do business with people, not companies. People email, text and send messages to people, not companies. The more you can sound like a real person, the better. The more you can let your true voice and personality come through, the better. Just think about what you would say if you were on the phone, instead of writing a message. Include all of the little editorializing phrases that speak to the results and emotions. For instance, if someone mentions that they're considering a May wedding, and your gardens are in full bloom in May, you might say:

"I'm so glad you're looking at May as our ceremony area and gardens are in full bloom. Your photos are going to be gorgeous!"

Oh, and beginning your message with: *"Congratulations on your recent engagement..."* seems like a nice way to start, but one of my clients secret-shopped all of his competitors and 85% of them began their messages that way. When you only see your message, it seems pleasant. When you're the customer and you see multiple messages starting that way, it's not so special anymore.

2. **Reply as quickly as you can** – Again, this sounds obvious and there are some very good reasons why you want to get back to them quickly. If you were the customer, and you had just sent an inquiry, whether through email, contact form, text, messaging, etc., how fast would you want a reply? While you may think that getting a reply within 24 hours is acceptable, you really want a reply faster. The faster you reply, the more likely they are still in shopping mode, looking at your site or the site they inquired through (The Knot, WeddingWire, social platform, etc.). If you reply later, they're likely to be doing something else (working, not in front of their computer, etc.). Another good reason is that a WeddingWire survey had shown that couples said they chose the first wedding pro to reply 50% of the time! While I'd like you to be the first to reply, I know it isn't always possible. With the tips in this book you can be the one who replies the best!

3. **Mirror their tone** – When people write to you, they use either a formal or casual tone. If they start with: *"To whom it may concern. We would like to inquire about using your services*

for our impending nuptials", that would be a very formal tone. On the other hand, if you get: *"OMG, my BFF and I are getting MARRIED!!!"*, that would be a very casual tone. We do business with people we feel comfortable with, and mirroring their tone reduces or eliminates another friction point. If they write formally to you, and you reply casually, that's friction. You also don't want to come across as unprofessional by sounding too casual when they're writing formally to you. When working with corporate customers, you're still dealing with people, not the company. Mirror the tone of the person you're communicating with.

4. **Mirror their energy** – related to their tone is their energy. How excited do they sound? Are they using a lot of exclamation points to show that they are excited? Are they using emoticons/emojis (👍,♥)? I try to wait until the other person uses emojis and then I may use some back. If they don't think that you're excited about doing their wedding or event, they'll find someone else who is. There are times when it's hard to judge their excitement level. Make sure you're mirroring their tone (#3) even when you can't feel the energy.

5. **Mirror how much they write** – Have you noticed that some people write you sound-bites or phrases, not full sentences? And other people write you long stories with lots and lots of details, often when it's not necessary. Those are signals to you. When someone is writing you short replies, you should mirror that style. People who write short answers to you don't usually want to read long replies. Conversely, when someone writes you longer messages, it's a signal that it's OK to write longer answers. You don't

have to, but they're more likely to read a longer answer than someone who writes you short replies.

A note about contact forms: If you get a lot of your inquiries through contact forms, whether on your website or another platform, it's likely that you won't know if they're going to write long or short replies, as the contact form removes their tone, energy and many don't write much of a message, if they write anything in the message box at all. Don't get me wrong, I think contact forms are great, the shorter the better. Statistically, the longer the form, less people will fill it out, even if all of the fields aren't required. Shorten the form and more people will fill it out. Only ask what you need to know to start the conversation. I'll talk more about this in a later chapter.

One of the best tips is to try to fit your messages on one screen of a smartphone. Unless or until they write you a long message, writing short messages gives you a better chance of them being read. Do you like to read long messages on your phone (or even on your laptop or desktop)? Probably not, and neither do your couples and clients. People tend to scan before they read (if they read the whole message at all). Writing messages that can be read on one screen give you a better chance of getting them read.

6. **Don't answer questions they haven't yet asked you** – this is a basic rule of selling and something I covered in "Shut Up and Sell More Weddings & Events." When you're talking, everything you say you already know. Similarly, when you're writing, everything you write you already know. You're not learning anything about what they want and need. Just replying with a lot of information, some of

which may have already been on the website or marketing piece that they've already seen, is not a good tactic. That's like the salesperson in a store who goes on and on about features of a product without knowing if they are important to you. Or the waiter/waitress who goes into a long presentation about a particular dish before finding out if you even like that type of food.

6a) End each email with one question - My favorite tip from "Why Don't They Call Me?", and the one that has yielded the most immediate results to so many of you, is to end each email with one question. It came from a conversation I was having with Alan Katz, who has the largest company for wedding ceremonies in Southern California (if not the largest in the country). We were talking one day and he casually mentioned that he always has his people end each email with a question, because it gets them more replies. That was a light-bulb, a-ha moment! I credited him in the dedication of "Why Don't They Call Me?" I'll expand on this thought later in this book as it's that important.

7. **Don't send attachments ~~they haven't yet asked for~~** – when I started speaking on this topic, many years ago, I said to not send attachments they haven't yet asked for. That was before most people were reading their emails on mobile devices. There are lots of other good reasons why you shouldn't use attachments early in the conversation. I'll expand on this thought later in the book, as well.

8. **Don't stop the conversation if they haven't** – a lot of the focus of this book, and of "Why Don't They Call Me?" is about how and when to follow-up. Remember, you're like

a dog who's just been given a bone... don't let go so easily! Too many of you aren't following up enough (or maybe at all) which is leaving money on the table. You already got the inquiry. They need your product/service. Don't give up so soon. As I said earlier, it's much easier to keep working a lead you've already received, but have no resolution, than to get someone else to make an inquiry.

If you want more detail about each of these, you'll find it in "Why Don't They Call Me?" as well as in the rest of this book. While this is the sequel to that book, it doesn't matter which you read first. "Why Don't They Call Me?" was about how to reply. This book fills in the blanks for when they're not replying as often, or as well as you'd like.

EVERYTHING WORKS SOME OF THE TIME,
NOTHING WORKS ALL OF THE TIME

One of the things that stops us from trying something new is that what we're already doing works, at least some of the time. The way that you've been replying to inquiries has gotten you good results, some of the time. Maybe it's even gotten you good results much of the time. However, if it was getting you good results most or all of the time, and you're filling your calendar with good-paying couples/clients, you probably wouldn't be reading this book. The way we interact with our customers and prospect changes over time. Over the 25+ years I've been around the wedding and events industry, about every five years we've had to adapt in some way to our customers communication style/method. Whether it was going from phone to email, or email to messaging and texting, or just that we're dealing with a different generation of customer, things can and will change.

I've made this admission before: I'm a 'digital-immigrant'. It's not a problem or handicap, it's just a statement of fact. Much of the technology that we use today just wasn't around when I started in this industry. I had a cell phone, but service was spotty and expensive. I was more likely to use a pay phone to call my clients from the road. Don't get me wrong, I love technology. I'm an early-adopter of many new technologies and I'll upgrade and replace my tech when I think the benefits outweigh the invest-ment. My smartphone has many apps for communicating with clients that I didn't use five or ten years ago (WhatsApp, Face-book Messenger App, ZipWhip for texting, etc.). I've added more as you, my clients, have started using them. Five years ago Twitter was a much-used app for me. Now, I'm more likely to be on Insta-gram than on Twitter.

If you're holding on to "the way things used to be", you're being left behind. Today's couples are Gen Y (millennials) and even Gen Z. Many of the people who inquire from companies are also Gen Y and Gen Z. These are 'digital-natives'. They were born into a world with most of the technologies we now use. My two Gen Y sons have never known a world without cell phones or personal computers. They might remember the early days of texting, but for them, it's always been around. If you're not Gen Y or Z, you might have had to learn to adapt to their preferred communica-tion methods. Having a conversation through their fingertips is normal, they've been doing it their whole lives. And remember that it's the customer who chooses the communication method.

In the Opportunity Cost chapter, I said that your real profit potential lies with the prospects and customers who already made an inquiry but are not currently replying. In other words, with the ones where the methods you're currently trying aren't working. As I mentioned in that chapter, if you're getting half of the people who are inquiring to engage in a meaningful conversation with you now, it's the other half where you can gain the most additional sales and profit. They have already reached out which means they need your product or service. They have already cut down the huge list of potential suppliers of your product/service to a very small list, and you're on it. It's way easier to convert a few more of those leads than to try to get more people to make new inquiries.

Don't be fooled by the success you have with some people and blame your prospects for not replying to you. Almost everything works some of the time. Don't worry, you won't have to totally scrap everything you do, but a few tweaks here and there can make a huge difference. And fair warning, nothing works all of the time. So, even if you follow everything I say in this book and "Why Don't They Call Me?", you'll still get ghosted by some of them. Nothing works all of the time. I wish I had a 100% guarantee for you, but it's inevitable that some people just won't reply, even just to tell you they've booked someone else.

They key is to reduce the number of people with whom you don't get a resolution, a yes or no. For most of you, a few more ghosts that become yesses each month or each year can add a lot to your bottom line. It's also a process that may need some experimenting. What works with some people may not work with others. If you have more than one tool in your replying toolbox, you'll be better equipped to get more and better replies. I was working with a client recently and gave him two different initial replies to try. I suggested that he alternate them for a while and see which works better. Then, he can just use that one. You may have to let go of a few of your favorite go-to reply techniques. You won't know if something else works better unless you give it a real try. That can feel a little scary, taking that leap of faith. But again, since you're reading this book, you understand that you can get a better response than you're getting now. And I'm happy to be your guide.

NOTES

NOT ALL LEADS ARE CREATED EQUAL

You need to consider where your leads are coming from, as not all leads are created equal. If you get an inquiry from someone who was the Maid of Honor at a wedding you did, that's very different than someone who Googled: "wedding décor near me." If you get an inquiry from someone who was referred to you for a corporate event, that's different than someone searching online for a: "photo booth company near me." Your success with leads from different sources can and will vary, as it should. You need to make sure you're not unfairly comparing results (ROI – return on investment) from different sources and considering them equal. Your results from different ad platforms will be different, even if the platforms seem similar.

I have clients who are on both websites: The Knot and WeddingWire. Some get similar results from both, and some get very different results. It's not right or wrong, it's just different. When you consider that the couples who are inquiring through The Knot are not the same as those inquiring through WeddingWire, it's the combined response that matters. I've seen too many wedding and event pros drop an ad, or stop going to a wedding show only to see their inquiries drop. Often, you don't know where your leads are coming from, or how many other things influenced them before they reached out. In "Shut Up and Sell More Weddings &

Events" I wrote that marketing is like a relay race. Just as the runners pass the baton from one to the other as the race progresses, your couples and clients are moving from one form of exposure to you to another, and then another, and then another... until they make their inquiry. For some of them it's a short race, just a few steps. For others there will be many steps, and even starts and stops along the way.

When you're looking at your conversion from lead to sale, take into account the different lead sources. You'll never know them all as you have no visibility to many of them. You can't see when someone visits your website and doesn't make an inquiry. You can't see when someone goes to Guides for Brides and doesn't click on your listing. You can't see who's at the wedding expo and chooses not to stop at your booth. While some of that is somewhat trackable, if you really want to know and are willing to do the work, most of us don't know that someone is even in the market for what we do until we get the inquiry.

When it comes to getting the attention of prospects, I like to be as diversified as possible. As I said in the chapter on: "The 4 Steps to More Sales", you want to be everywhere your prospective couples and clients are when they're looking for someone like you. I don't like having all of my eggs in one basket. Too many wedding and event pros found out the hard way, during the pandemic lock downs, that some of their sources of leads had dried up. If your connections at other vendors were no longer at those other businesses, or if those businesses weren't seeing any customers, a source of leads for you dried up. Networking is great, but it's fueled by seeing and interacting with people. You do that at networking events. You do that by seeing each other at weddings and events. You need to stoke those relationships, not let them die out.

If you've done any online shopping, you're familiar with recommendation engines. That's when you're looking at a product and you're offered other, similar products: "If you like this, you might also like..." Sometimes you look at those suggestions and sometimes you don't. If you're already sure of what you want, you might not even consider those suggestions. However, if you're still open to other choices, you might give them a look. In the wedding and event world, if a couple/customer looks at an ad online, they might also be offered other suggestions. Sometimes they'll take a look, and sometimes they won't. Searches on Google often start with paid ads before you get to the organic results. On some websites, if the couple/customer makes an inquiry they might be offered to also reach out to other, similar suppliers. Some couples/customers do it, some don't.

Those suggested or recommended suppliers will get leads that weren't originally asking about them. While the conversion rate on those secondary recommendations might be lower than primary ones, many of them can and do convert to conversations and sales. Don't treat them any differently. All inquiries are good ones until proven otherwise. If you don't reply at all, you're taking yourself out of the game. You have an almost 0% chance of making that sale. If a couple/customer feels that you're just going through the motions with the way you reply (maybe a copy/pasted reply that looks and feels generic), that's a good reason for them to ghost you. You need to seem just as interested in working with them as they are with having you be a part of their wedding or event.

So, when you're analyzing your results – you are analyzing your results, aren't you? – look at the trending of that particular source of leads over time. Don't unfairly compare leads from different sources. What should you be tracking? Ideally, I'd like you to know how many inquiries you get from each source. Then, how many of those you were able to have a conversation with (digital or otherwise). Then, how many of those went to the next step, which for many is likely to be a phone call, Zoom call, in-person meeting or tour. And then, of course, how many become sales. You should also be tracking how many you didn't get because you were already booked. Those were still good leads and the ad/source worked for you. If you find that you're getting a lot of leads for dates you're already booked, that's a sign that you may have pricing power for some of your more popular dates, or maybe it's time to think about expanding. If you're not keeping track of that, you won't see the patterns over time.

If you're getting a lot of leads that aren't converting, there are a few other reasons why that could be. Of course, one of them is how you're replying and following up (that is, if you're following up). This book will certainly help improve that. But another possibility is that you're just not getting good, qualified leads. Many of my clients were getting leads that weren't converting and it was because they had no pricing information on their websites, so they were actually encouraging anyone to reach out, regardless of their budgets. Just remember the times when you were the customer and there was no pricing on a website. What did you do? Sometimes you left and looked elsewhere. Sometimes you reached out and asked about pricing. Asking about price doesn't mean you can't afford it. It doesn't mean you want the cheapest thing they sell. It just means that you're interested enough to want to get an idea of pricing. I'll talk more about pricing and about pricing on websites in later chapters.

It's the same for your couples and clients. If there's no pricing info at all on your website/ads/marketing, you're missing out on some good leads with the people that leave without contacting you. And you're encouraging inquiries from people who can't afford you, or don't want to spend what you charge - just because they can afford it doesn't mean they have you high enough on their priorities list to pay your prices. I'll discuss the four ways to handle price inquiries later in the book. Suffice it to say, for now, that transparency leads to trust, which leads to better inquiries. Many of you would like to get fewer, but better inquiries. I agree! That would give you more time to follow-up better with the more qualified leads. Having better, clearer pricing info (not necessarily a price list or all of your prices) is one way to help you get both fewer and more qualified leads.

As I was writing this chapter, I got an email from a wedding pro who shared a link to a Reddit post from a bride who was complaining: *"Why is the pricing so secretive with all of these vendors. Can we talk about why it is so difficult & secretive to get prices from vendors?"* At last count there were 269 comments on the post, and while I didn't read them all, the theme of them was pretty clear from the start. The lack of transparency and pressing couples to have a call, meeting or come for a tour, to get a price, was chasing them away. If you'd like to see the post, here's a link: bit.ly/3blWdZA

NOTES

Email and WhatsApp and Texting, Oh My!

S ince we're working with so many digital natives, we also have to contend with the many forms of digital communication. As I mentioned in the Preface, I know that it would be so much easier for so many of you if they would just pick up the phone and call you. Sometimes I wonder why we call our devices 'smart phones', when it seems like the least used part of those devices is the phone! We have to accept that the customer gets to decide which way they want to reach out to us. And if we don't offer their preferred method, they just might pass us by. That doesn't mean that you have to offer every type available, but you don't want to create unnecessary friction by not having the most common and expected methods.

I mentioned earlier about a wedding pro who only offered calling or texting, no email or contact form. That's friction. Like it or not, people are comparing your website experience with all other websites they visit, not just others in your market and category, and not just ones for weddings/events. Not having a contact form and/or a way to email someone when you're on their website just seems odd. You would expect to at least be able to email them. What are some of the other ways to communicate that you may want to add to your website or marketing mix:

- **Texting** – you can either use your cell phone, or a third-party service so they can text without having your mobile number, and so your team can text without giving their numbers. I use ZipWhip (ZipWhip.com) which lets people text my office number (which is a landline, not a mobile number). I can access the texts through my cell phone, desktop, laptop and tablet. Another advantage is that if you or your co-worker/employee are unavailable, someone else can reply. And if an employee leaves, they don't take the message history with them on their personal cell phone.

- **Facebook Messenger** – there's an app you can add to your site as well as direct messages through your Facebook page

- **WhatsApp** – this is much more popular outside the United States. I started using it as my international travel increased and I then added mention of WhatsApp on some marketing pieces and in my books. This is a perfect example of me following the lead of my customers and prospects to a method of communication.

- **Messaging through your ad platforms** – The Knot, WeddingWire, weddingsonline, EasyWeddings, Guides for Brides and many other sites like them around the world have their own messaging platforms. Some have mobile apps for it as well. On some you can reply through your regular email, on others you have to reply through their app/site.

- **Other social media platform messaging** – If you have a presence on Instagram, YouTube, LinkedIn, Pinterest, etc., there's a good chance someone may send you a message there. It's very important that you pay attention to those as you could miss out on some good leads if you don't keep an eye on them.

- **Live chatting on your site** – I've seen a lot of wedding and event pros who offer their website visitors the option of chatting live with a company representative. This allows an instant, real-time conversation, without them having to call you. If they're in their office, they may be able to chat with you through your site, but not pick up the phone (and get busted by the boss and their co-workers for planning their wedding/event from work). My only caution here is to be clear about when you are, or are not, available to chat. You don't want someone to decide to reach out that way only to find out there's no one to chat with now. One of my clients has it so that the chat feature doesn't even appear unless they're available to chat now. On sites for some large companies the chat isn't with a person, it's AI – artificial intelligence – trying to answer the most common queries. I have found some to be helpful, but most to be annoying as they can't answer my questions (I've probably already tried to find the answer before chatting).

With so many possible methods of communicating, how are you supposed to keep track of them all? That's a legitimate question and an equally real problem. My advice is to not give them any way to reach out that you aren't paying attention to. If they message you on Facebook and you don't reply, how much could that be costing you in lost profits? Many of you are connected with me through Facebook or LinkedIn. If you've told that platform your birthday, it notifies me, and everyone else you're connected, with when it's your birthday. It's very likely that you've received a Happy Birthday message from me, not on your wall, but in a private message. Since Facebook caps our profile's 'friends' at 5,000, I use this to help keep me below the cap. I'm perpetually at over 4,950 friends. If I wish you Happy Birthday in a private message, and you don't acknowledge it (I'm not looking for a long message back, just a reaction or 👍 will do), and this happens two years in a row, then I'll 'unfriend' you. That doesn't mean I don't like you. It's just an acknowledgement that you're not paying attention to that platform's messaging service. I understand that birthdays are busy times, and many of you, like me, get hundreds of birthday messages. I just need a way to reduce my friend count and I figure that after two years, it's pretty clear that your attention is elsewhere (and I do wait for a couple of weeks after the second message to give you time to catch up). I reply to every private message I get, so I'm not asking of others anything I don't do myself.

Is it OK to text them? The answer is Yes, but when you text them will vary. Some of you have a field for phone number on your contact form, with a box that says: "OK to text". That's called per-mission-based marketing. If they check the box, then it's perfectly fine to text them. Even if they didn't check the box, you're still replying to their inquiry where they gave you their phone number. That's very different than texting someone who hasn't reached out to you yet. Many wedding pros have told me that they're having great success with texting. That makes sense since the generations you're likely working with grew up texting their friends and family. Another good reason to text is that, according to ZipWhip, 90% of text messages are seen within 3 minutes of when they're received. That's way better than with emails.

If you do decide to text them, be sure to include who you are, as most texts don't have 'signatures' with name and contact infor-mation the way your emails do. As you'll see in a later chapter, I'm not a big fan of auto-replies (unless I'm truly out of the office), but on my ZipWhip texting I have an auto-reply that asks the sender to tell me who they are, if they haven't already done so. Most of the texts I get don't say who they are, so they're followed closely by a second text with their name (and sometimes company info). Most of the time I can't tell who they are if they weren't already in my contacts, and neither can your couples and clients.

One friend, who's company provides DJ and Photography services, has been having great success by replying to their inquiry via email, and then texting to tell them that they did. It goes something like this:

> *"Hi Stacy, this is Jamie from Acme DJ-Photo. I got your inquiry and just sent an email with some information. I can't wait to find out more about how we can make your wedding fun and capture your beautiful images. Take a look and then call, email or text, whichever is easier for you. Looking forward to connecting."*

I think because she isn't only texting it's having a different impact. And while some do text her back, she isn't specifically asking for a text reply. She gives them options. Another entertainment company called me in September 2020, mid-pandemic, to tell me that his sales have stayed steady all year (not dropping as it did for so many others), and that he attributes using texting almost exclusively to much of his success.

When I added texting as an option to my site and marketing materials, I was surprised when the first text I got wasn't from a millennial. It was actually a baby-boomer, who ended up hiring me to do a workshop. So, this isn't a generational thing. It's making it easier for all of your customers and prospects to choose how they want to connect with you. Which methods should you use on your website and in your marketing? Look to your customers to find out. Talk to your current and past customers and see if there are ways to reach out that you don't currently offer, and if those are ways they would use, or might have used. Again, that's why I started using WhatsApp. My international customers showed me it was their preferred way to communicate.

Just recently I got an email from someone who's been listening to my podcast and reading my books. He got a lead on Facebook and instead of trying to move them to email or phone or an in-person meeting, he continued the conversation on Facebook messenger. He followed my tips, asked good questions, listened to the answers and here's the result:

> *"Yesterday, a potential bride contacted me via FB messenger and using your techniques of listening and letting them tell me what they needed we were able to get a contract signed. I can't wait to use these techniques more."*

Every method of communication is just that... communicating. Don't try to force them to other methods, at least not right away (more on that later). It's a big reason for them to ghost you. You also don't need to offer them all of the possible ways to communicate, but you do need to pay attention to any of the ways you choose to offer. I've heard of more than one wedding/event pro who wasn't getting their leads from some sources because of technical issues. Or maybe the email address that the leads were coming in to wasn't being monitored. I remember secret-shopping a venue client after I did sales training for them (at his request). We didn't get a reply, so we reached out both through their website and one of their ads (The Knot or WeddingWire). We still didn't get a reply, which was very strange given the training we had just done. It turned out that the leads were coming to an email address of a former employee that no one was monitoring. That was many tens of thousands of dollars in missed opportunities. I just heard the same thing from a rental company client. The leads were going to the email address of a former employee, and no one was checking that inbox. A photographer once told me that Gmail was routing many of his website's leads to a "promotions" folder (one that he didn't know existed) so he missed out on many of his inquiries for over a year! You might want to check all of your lead sources and make inquiries to see that they're all coming through. I'll talk more about how and when you can move someone from one method of communication to another, later in this book.

NOTES

IS YOUR CONTACT FORM DISCOURAGING INQUIRIES?

aving a contact form on your website is a must. It's an easy way for someone to reach out any time of the day or night. I've actually added a short contact form to every page of my website (except the homepage). That way you can reach out to me without leaving the page. You can email, call, text or use the short contact form on every page. Like you, I struggled with how many fields to use on my contact forms. There's a balance between what you need to know *ever*, and what you need to know *now*. Too many wedding and event pro's contact forms are too long. There are a few reasons why this could be a bad idea. One of those reasons is that adding fields reduces the number of people who will fill out the form at all, even if those fields aren't required.

A quick look online to see how many fields a contact form should have landed me on the WPForms.com website. They have a post: "14 Form Conversion Best Practices (Backed by Research)". In it they say: *"The last thing you want to do is overwhelm the user. If you can help it, never include more than 3 fields on your form. According to Quicksprout, limiting the number of fields to just 3 can guarantee a minimum conversion rate of 25%. Another study by Hubspot verifies this concept, showing that reducing the number of fields from 4 to 3 brings a 50% improvement in form completion."*

A post on the MySiteAuditor.com website said that: *"NeilPatel. com was able to increase conversions by 26% by removing 1 field from his contact form."*

So, here we have the push and pull to add or remove fields from your contact forms. Before you go adding more questions to your contact form to get more qualified inquiries, think about what you could be missing out on. Someone has already gotten to your website. They're interested enough to go to your contact form. If your form is too long (especially on a mobile device) and they decide to leave your site, you're missing the chance to have a conversation with them at all. If you can fill your calendar with the people who now fill out your longer form, then there's no problem. But if you're either not getting enough leads, or not getting the right leads, or not converting enough of the leads, then a shorter form might be the ticket for you.

I was consulting for a client, a 5-Star, all-inclusive resort in Mexico. They added more questions to their destination wedding contact form, thinking that it would better qualify their inquiries. While it's true that the people that fill out that longer form would be qualified, it would also reduce their number of inquiries, which was going against their goal. I also suggested that since their target clientele (high net-worth couples) are busy with their businesses and lives, they may not want to answer many of the questions on the form, just to get some information. There's a fine balance here.

Should you ask for their phone number at all and/or make it a required field? In the WPForms.com article they say: *"If there's one piece of information users hate giving away, it's their phone num-bers. **Research shows that asking for a phone number leads to high form abandonment in almost every situation.**"* In other words, instead of giving you their phone number, they just go away and look at your competitors. How do you feel when you're the customer and the contact form asks for your phone number? Does it sometimes feel intrusive? I can remember a few times where I filled out an online contact form, looking for information, only to get a phone call minutes later. It felt intrusive. I could have called them for information. Instead, I chose to use their contact form because it was more convenient for me to send a message at that time, than to speak on the phone. For your wedding/event business I think it's OK to ask for the phone number, I just wouldn't make it a required field. Just remember, it's not whether *you* want their phone number. It's also how many people might not fill out your form and contact you, at all, if you make it required. If you get a lot of people putting bogus phone numbers (like 000-000-0000, or 123-456-7890), that's a sign that some of your prospects would rather not give you their numbers, yet, and that you may be missing out on inquiries from people who abandoned the contact form when they saw the phone number was required.

Another reason I don't like longer contact forms is that I want you to leave some low-commitment questions for when you're having a conversation with them, whether digitally, on the phone/Zoom or in-person. As you'll see later in this book, asking their guest count, or wedding location, or for venues the date they want, takes away questions you can ask to get them to reply to you more quickly. If your website has done its job – and for most of you its main job is to get you the inquiry – then having a shorter contact form would be a good idea, so you convert more of that site traffic to inquiries. While I have a short contact form on every page, I also have a separate Contact Page. The link is on my navigation menu all the way to the right. Why? Because instinctively that's where people look when they want to find a Contact Page. Burying it in a drop down menu or naming it something else is going to add friction. Why do I need a contact page if there's a form on every page? Some people might come to my site looking for how to contact me. And while there is contact info at the top of every page, and throughout all of my pages, if they just look to the top right corner, or the bottom of my mobile menu, they'll find it, right where they expect it to be, reducing the friction!

9 Reasons you're getting ghosted, and how to fix them!

In the following chapters I'm going to share nine common reasons why you're getting ghosted and how you can help to minimize them. You'll notice that I didn't say eliminate them, because it's just not realistic to say that you'll never get ghosted. While there are surely other reasons, these 9 are very common for wedding and event pros, like you. What I can tell you, from my experience with wedding and event pros just like you, is that if you follow these tips, as well as what you may have already heard or read from me, you will get ghosted less. This applies to wedding inquiries as well as corporate and social event inquiries. You have to approach this with the right attitude. I've had many people tell me that they're following what I wrote in "Shut Up and Sell More Weddings & Events" and/or "Why Don't They Call Me?" and it's not working. When I have the opportunity to see what they're actually doing, they may be doing some of these things, but still doing others the same way as they did before.

You wouldn't paint half of a room and say you're finished or put on one shoe and say that you're dressed. If you're on a diet to lose weight, eating one less cookie is good. Learning how to eat differently, a lifestyle change, is better. And similarly, you need to be all-in on trying some new things with the way you communicate.

There's an old saying: *"If you always do what you've always done, you'll always get what you've always gotten."* You also have to keep an open mind. If you want different results than what you're getting now, you have to be open to new ideas. To paraphrase Henry Ford: *"Whether you think you can, or whether you think you cannot, you're right!"* If you think you can't learn anything new, then you might as well stop reading now. This, as with most new things, is a trial-and-error process. Try something new, see how it works, tweak what you're doing and try again. You might also find that different strategies work with leads from different sources. I worked with one company on specific wording for his leads from a venue, who gave him the list of couples who had booked that venue (he's one of their preferred suppliers). Because they were warmer leads than some of his other inquiries, we used the same methods, but with different wording. We referenced the venue that was referring them as well as the work he's done there before (with reviews and, at times, relevant photos from weddings he did at that venue).

If you use a one-size-fits-all approach, you'll get a more generic response. People can tell when they're getting a pre-written, copy-pasted response versus a personal one. No matter how personal you think your copy-pasted response is, when you see it as your prospects do, compared to the many other replies they've gotten, from other wedding and event pros in your category, and from other categories of vendors, many of them start to look the same. We do a lot of secret-shopping in my consulting, both of my clients' businesses as well as their competitors. We see hundreds of responses from wedding and event pros around the world each year. Way too many look very similar. And when I talk to those people, I find out that they think they had done a good job of personalizing. Using technology to merge in their wedding date or other data is a good idea. How and where you do it will change how it looks and feels to your couples and clients. Just think about the emails and messages that you get when you're the consumer or prospective customer. Can't you tell when something feels more generic from when it's truly personalized? OK, let's get to 9 Reasons You're Getting Ghosted!

NOTES

REASON #1:
YOU GAVE THEM WHAT
THEY THINK THEY NEED

Many of your inquiries look very similar to these:

- *Hey there! We are interested in potentially hosting our wedding at your venue. Could you send through information on your **packages**? Thanks!*

- *Hi, we saw you on (website/social platform) and were wondering if you're available on (date) and what **packages** you offer?*

- *Hi, could you please send over information about your **prices** and **packages**? Thank you!*

This seems pretty straight forward, right? They're asking to see your pricing and packages, so why not just send them over? Well, there's more going on here than just their words. First, you need to look at where that inquiry is coming from. What information is on that site, page or marketing piece? What might they have already seen, read, watched, heard or experienced before they made their inquiry? Did they type that inquiry or just choose the default text offered by that platform? As you've noticed, many of them take the path of least friction and use the generic, default text. Do they really want packages and pricing information? Yes, however that's probably not all they want or need to know in order to see that you're the best choice for their wedding or event. Unless your USP – Unique Selling Proposition – is that you're the lowest-priced option, sending all of your prices before having a conversation with them is just giving them a license to shop you against other choices.

Before you start sending things over to them, it would be good to know what they might already know about you. Of course, it's impossible to know everything they already know about you, but clearly whatever they do know is positive enough for them to want to know more. Your couples and clients take many steps before they reach out to you. Even if they contact you from your business card or brochure, you would want to know where and when they got that piece to really know where your business is coming from. If they have your printed brochure, or it's available through your website, it would be redundant to email them a PDF of that same piece when they make an inquiry. That's not moving the conversation forward. If they've been to your website, which presumably has a lot of information about your business, it might also be redundant to send them a PDF of a brochure with very similar information.

Remember that by the time you get an inquiry they've eliminated most of your competitors. They've looked at as many choices as they could find, but it was too many to choose from – which is called the: "Paradox of Choice" (also the book I mentioned earlier). When we're the consumer we want to know that we've seen all of the available choices. However, we live in a world where there are usually way too many choices, which makes the decision process harder. Yes, having more choices is generally better, but it makes it harder to ultimately decide. So, we have to start filtering our choices, eliminating other options until we get down to a more manageable set of choices. That's what you're doing on sites like Amazon.com and others when you use their filters. If you're like me, I click the "Prime" button on Amazon first, to limit my choices to the ones with Prime Shipping. That cuts the choices, but also still leaves many, many options. Then you might choose to filter by the ratings, or the color, manufacturer and/or price range.

Before you get an inquiry, your couples and clients have gone through a similar process of filtering... and you've made the cut. How many others in your market and category are still in the running? In a perfect world it would be just you. And that may happen if they've had prior experience with you and your product/service. If a company comes back to you each year to do their holiday party, without shopping around, that's great! With weddings it's not as easy. Even if they've experienced what you do, they still may look to see what else is available. Their boss, or a committee, may require that they look at other options each year. You still have an advantage with them, but it's not a guarantee of a sale. Referrals are better than cold leads, but they're not always going to go with you. They might have also been referred to, or personally experienced other wedding and event pros at other weddings and events (friends, family, corporate events, fund-raisers, etc.).

What I've heard over the years, both from couples and from surveys from The Knot, WeddingWire and The Wedding Report, is that couples will narrow their lists to three to five choices in most categories. Some will certainly have more, and some will have less. Just remember that people research, shop and buy in different ways. A close friend of ours has two millennial (Gen Y) sons. When the older one got married, he and his fiancée did a lot of researching for each service. For instance, they narrowed their list of DJs to three that the venue referred and two others that they found on their own. Three years later, when his younger brother was getting married, they did their online research and reached out, in many cases, to only the one that they decided they wanted. The visited one venue and booked it. They spoke to one videographer and booked them. The bride saw a gown in a store window that she liked, and she bought it. That's the way their wedding planning went.

Once you get the inquiry, your job is to continue the conversation that the customer has already started with you. You're not trying to start a conversation, it's already been started. The last thing you'd want to do is chase the customer away at this point. Give them a reason to want to continue having a conversation with you, not ghost you. And when I say: "conversation", that refers to any way of communicating, including all of the digital methods (email, messaging, texting, WhatsApp, etc.).

Why is sending them your packages, especially when that's what their messages asks, a reason for you to get ghosted? There are a few reasons. First, it's not necessarily what they really want, but they don't know how to articulate that you to. It's very likely that they've never shopped for your product or service before, so they don't know how to shop for it. When we're the consumer and we've never shopped for a particular product or service, we often default to asking about price. Price is a common denominator for all of us because there will be a transaction, with an exchange of money, at some point. And in case I don't say this later in the book, there may be a transaction, but you don't have to make it feel transactional. They will pay attention to the whole experience of doing business with you and others, not just the list of products, services and prices. By the time they reach out to you they're signaling that they need your product or service. You don't need to sell them, you need to help them buy. If you make it transactional, you're commoditizing what you do and letting it be all, or mostly about the price. If you make it more personal, you're showing them a glimpse of how you'll work with them when they choose you.

I worked with a client on how he replies to inquiries, and he had been sending a link to a hidden page on his site with his pricing and packages (a hidden page is a page on your website that you can't get to without having the direct link. There are no links on the rest of the website to take you there). He came to me because he wasn't converting enough of his leads, and he also wanted me to review his pricing and packages. I recommended that he stop sending a link to the pricing page as it was giving them a license to shop his packages and prices against his competitors. He wasn't getting a chance to sell them on choosing him and the results that only he can provide (more on selling the results later). He was reluctant, at first, as he wanted them to know his prices so he could filter out the ones that can't afford him, but he wasn't ready to put his pricing on his site. I gave him two options for the wording for his messaging, one with a price range and one with no price (you'll find some examples of this later in the book). I said he should try alternating the two messages to see which converts better, and then use that one. We finalized the wording for his messages a week ago. As of when I'm writing this, his conversion has gone up, dramatically and he's been emailing me the success stories of the couples he's booking using the ideas in this book. It was a big change from what he was doing before, and the results are going right to his bottom line! Here's what he just wrote to me: *"Thanks again and I'm excited about how couples are now responding!"*

Sending them a brochure and/or prices, right away, is encouraging them *not* to reply now because the implication is that the information they need is in that brochure or price list. If you make an inquiry with a business and they send you a brochure and/or price list, you're going to want to check out what they sent before replying. That delay in getting back to you is the ghosting. And *you* caused it by sending them that document. And if they open that document, which they may, or may not, and it's just a repeat of what they already know about you, some might move on to other choices. Maybe it's because they feel you're being evasive or redundant. Every time you interact with someone you should be adding value. Sending them things they already know isn't adding value, it's adding frustration and friction.

Another reason that attachments can cause ghosting is that their spam filter might block it or send it to a 'Junk' folder. Every one of us has a Junk folder (or something similar) in our email, and very often things that we actually want end up there. It's hard to list all the reasons why an email program thinks something is spam, but having attachments is definitely one of them. Even without attachments, many emails you send will end up not making it to their inboxes. Whether it's a spam filter, Promotions folder (Gmail), Clutter folder (Outlook) or Junk folder, there's just no way to ensure that every email makes it through. That's one reason why it's important to use the messaging services (Facebook, The Knot, WeddingWire, WhatsApp, etc.) when the couple/customer uses that to reach out to you. Those messaging services don't have the same types of junk filters as email programs, ensuring that your message makes it through. Making it to their Inbox doesn't mean they'll read it. But getting it to their messaging inbox is infinitely better than having it diverted to a Junk folder. As I said in the recap of "Why Don't They Call Me?", first use the method that they used to inquire with you before trying another method. But if they don't reply, as you'll read in Reason #8, you have to at least try one other method before even thinking of giving up.

According to WeddingWire over 70% of couples are reading their consumer emails on mobile devices. I would guess that most people these days, regardless of whether it's for work or personal use are reading much if not most of their emails on mobile devices. Those PDF brochures and documents you send them will just shrink down to their small screen size. That's not a good user experience. Here's a good exercise for you: send yourself, and maybe some friends and colleagues, an email with the same attachment(s) and open it/them on your phone. First see if it went to your Junk folder. Then open the attachment and see what it looks like. Can you read the text without 'pinching' to zoom in? Can someone with less than perfect eyesight read it at all?

If they do read your brochure, it's not going to make a sale for you. You need them to reach back out to you after reading it, or you need to follow-up to get in contact with them. The brochure stalls the process. You need to move the conversation forward towards a conversation and sale. Brochures and price lists don't make sales unless you're doing e-commerce. If they can't go to your website and make an actual purchase, then the best your site can do is get them to make an inquiry. But they've already made an inquiry, and now you want to send them away and have them come back and make another inquiry? I'm feeling the friction in the process building. I'll say it again, brochures don't make sales. People make sales. In the wedding and event industry, as with most businesses, it's people buying from people.

I want you to imagine that I've temporarily broken your attachment buttons. Treat digital inquiries the same as if they had called you. If someone calls you, I don't think you're going to take their email address and send them a brochure or price list before having a conversation with them. You have them on the phone... talk to them. Treat a digital inquiry the same. You have them in a conversation, keep it going! Don't attach anything, yet. And yes, I said "yet" because later in the conversation there *may* be a better time to send them something. Don't use it as a crutch to try to speed up the process. If you can get to the appointment or sale without attaching anything, and believe me, you can, then please resist attaching anything, especially on the initial reply.

REASON # 2:
YOU SENT THEM AWAY

Don't include any links in your initial reply. No links to your social media pages. No links to your ads and reviews. No links to your videos or photo galleries. No links to hidden pricing pages. As with Reason #1, anything that moves them farther away from you is working against your goal. Your goal at this point is to have a good conversation that leads to either an appointment/meeting/tour or a sale. Now I can feel some of you twitching uncomfortably already. No attachments and now no links? Come on, Alan, give us a break! I hear you and I feel your pain. But you're here to learn new ways to get ghosted less, right? Let's go back to the phone call scenario. Someone calls and asks for information. Instead of having a conversation right now with them, you tell them to go to your website, or your social channels, or your YouTube or Vimeo channel. Sounds silly when I say it that way, doesn't it?

All of those links are distractions. You've already gotten them to make an inquiry. Do you know if they've seen your social channels yet? Maybe – only if the inquiry came through there. Do you know if they've been to your website yet? Maybe - only if the inquiry came through there. Do you know if they've seen any of your videos? Maybe – only if the inquiry came through YouTube or a page where you have videos online. Have they seen any of your photos? Almost certainly, since most platforms will have photos, and since we're all more likely to look at the photos before we read the text. Do you need to send them away to see more photos in your initial reply? No.

If you send them to your social channels, you risk losing their attention. They might see things that aren't as interesting to them as whatever they've already seen – which got them to inquire. They are also just one click away from your competitors. When you're having a digital conversation with someone, you have a monopoly on their attention, even if it's for a few seconds. They're "talking" to you, not your competitor. Send them to Facebook, Instagram, Pinterest, TikTok, etc. and they can be looking at your competitor's page and content very easily. Some platforms will even suggest similar pages (your competitors) using the recommendation engines mentioned earlier – "If you like this, you might also like…".

This is why I don't even put links to my social platforms on my own website. I have sharing links, so if there's an article or product you want to 'share' on your social channels, you can do that. But you don't leave my site when you share. A window pops up and you type your message, click to post it and then close the window. You're still on the same place and page on my site. If you leave and go to that other site, you may not come back.

The only time I send people to YouTube is if they want to watch my podcast, the Wedding Business Solutions podcast. At the end of each episode it suggests other episodes, not other people's videos. There's a page on my site, Podcast.AlanBerg.com that has links to all of the podcast platforms. Those links take you right to my Channel on Apple Podcast, Google Podcast, Spotify,

Pandora, iHeartRadio, YouTube etc. Of course, you don't even have to leave that page to hear episodes. They're all listed right on that page, with a player app, and if you don't have a preferred podcast app, you can just click and hear them where you already are. Regular podcast listeners have a preferred podcast app and would be more likely to want to hear or watch them on that platform. If you do click any of those links, the window on my website stays open so you can easily pick up where you left off.

Even without having any links to my social channels on my website, I get new connection requests every day on Facebook, LinkedIn and Instagram (which, as of this writing, are the three platforms I pay the most attention to, because those are the ones my target audience use). Those are organic connections, with people who have found out about me some other way than already being on my website. If you're on my website, at this very moment I don't care if you know which social channels I'm on. I want you to make an inquiry about a service, buy one or more of my books, and more recently, find out that I have a podcast and listen to one or more episodes (and then subscribe so you hear about the new episodes).

Think of your social channels as feeders of traffic *to* your website, not the other way around. Your email and other digital replies should be the same. Their mission is to get the person who's already inquired, to continue the conversation that their inquiry has started. Links are another reason you could be getting ghosted. As with attachments, links have also been known to trigger spam filters. A quick Google search for: "what triggers spam filters" returns lots of results (161,000,000 results!). The email platform Constant Contact has a post that says: *"Sending from a free email address (Gmail, Yahoo, AOL, etc.) can cause an email to be delivered to the spam folder."* There were several other similar comments on the first page of that Google search. As to links triggering spam filters, here's something I hadn't realized: *"It's common for spammers to make it look like you're clicking on a link for one thing, but it's actually a link to something else, and spam filters look for this. Even something innocent, like a text link that says 'Please visit our website at www.mikeslandscaping.com', but the URL portion is linked to "www.mikeslandscaping.com/home", can be seen as spam."* You might have: *"Visit our Instagram Page"* as the text, and the link goes to your Instagram page, and that might trigger the spam filter. If you want to read more from their post visit: https://bit.ly/3v9SUwr (please, just finish reading this book first 👍).

Anything that distracts your couples and clients from replying back to you, right now, is working against you. Might there be a time, later in the conversation, where you may want to share something that you've posted, or a relevant video? Sure. Just not at the beginning of the conversation. You want to give them reasons to reply now, and links are reasons to go somewhere else, instead of replying.

Reason #3:
You asked for a call
or meeting in your first reply

OK, I know this is going to be controversial for many of you. I get it. I've heard this from wedding and event pros, just like you, over and over again. You want to get them on a phone/ Zoom call or to an in-person meeting or tour. You tell me: *"If I can get them on the phone or in-person, my closing ratio is fantastic!"* I don't doubt that for a minute. However, that's what *you* want. If that's what your couple or client wanted, they would have called you, instead of making a digital inquiry. Many of you have a link on your website to a calendar app, where they can schedule an appointment without contacting you first. That's a great option, just don't make it the only option. Not everyone is ready for that high-commitment action when they're on your website. Hopefully, you have a link to call you on your website, although I still come across some sites that make it hard, or impossible, to find a phone number. If they had wanted to talk to you on the phone, they could have called you... but they didn't.

Asking them on your initial reply for a call or a meeting is another big reason you're getting ghosted. For all of you who tell me that you don't want to be "pushy" when selling, this is being pushy. They want to ease their way into the conversation with you and you want them to change the medium with which you're already communicating. How many different ways are there to contact you on your website, in your ads and on your social channels? Of all the ways that they could have chosen to connect with you, they picked one and inquired (email, contact form, text, messaging, etc.). Meet them where they are and don't add friction now by trying to change the technology they've chosen.

Some of you may be missing out on inquiries by not offering their preferred method of communicating. I did a webinar presentation for a group of wedding pros in India, and the organizer asked me to tell the attendees that they should use email or messaging, instead of WhatsApp, to communicate with their couples. I told them that I can't do that because it's not up to me. It's up to the engaged couples to drive the technology choices. I didn't use WhatsApp until I started traveling internationally. My clients and prospects kept asking: "What's your WhatsApp number?" None of my US or Canadian contacts use it, but almost all of my other international contacts use it, at least part of the time, to connect with me. Just this week I was using WhatsApp to message with clients in Ireland, Mexico and India.

I mentioned in an earlier chapter about a wedding pro who only has the option to call or text him on his website (so he doesn't get spam). He's absolutely missing out on inquiries from people who are already on his website, by not offering at least a contact form. If he doesn't want to let them email him directly, that's not so bad, but only if he gives them a way to send a message (a contact form), which he doesn't. His target audience are engaged couples, who are likely to be digital natives. We know that calling is probably the least likely way they want to reach out. Texting is more likely (which he does offer), but not for everyone. Some people still try to keep their texts to personal conversations with close friends and family. Some don't want you to have their mobile number, yet.

I've seen websites for wedding pros with buttons that say: "Call Us Now." Most of those buttons go to their Contact page. If it truly is "Call Us Now" then the button should offer to dial the number when you click it. If that's the only choice, you'll miss out on contacts from couples and clients who don't want to call you. Most of my inquiries come in through my short contact forms (on every page of my website) or through messaging on my social channels. I offer texting and direct emailing multiple times on every page of my site, and yet I get very few text inquiries or direct email inquiries. You, just like your couples and clients, are choosing the method that works best for you. If you're thinking about adding a live chat feature, first think about your availability, so you don't give the impression you can "chat now", if it's more likely that you can't.

Let me give you a little hope, you will be able to ask them for a call/Zoom or in-person meeting, appointment and/or tour... just not yet. We're going to earn that right by approaching this more gently. It's a little like when you're on the dating scene looking to meet someone new. Let's say you're in a bar and you see someone that you want to approach. There's a seat open next to them at the bar. You muster up your courage and walk over. They notice you and your eyes meet and you say: *"Excuse me, would you like to get married?"* That's a little aggressive, wouldn't you agree? Wouldn't it be better to start with: *"Excuse me, is this seat taken?"* If you get a good response, you can then continue the conversation. If you get a negative reaction, you can walk away (sulking and feeling rejected – just kidding, that would never happen to you!). The difference here is that they are the one who reached out to you. They're the one who's asking: "Is this seat taken?". You're more likely to get a better response if you do things a little differently... which, after all, is exactly why you're reading this book. So, take heart, you can ask for the call/Zoom or meeting/tour, just not in your first reply, because it's another reason you're getting ghosted.

Now I know that some of you are twitching a little hearing me say to not ask for the phone call or meeting. I hear you and I understand where that's coming from. So, let me throw you a bone to those of you that just can't bear the thought of replying without asking for the call or meeting. Send your messages the way I suggest in this book. Then, below your name, but above your email signature (if you're emailing), add a 'PS' (postscript):

PS: Want to arrange a call or meeting with us? Click this link for our easy calendar app

Or try:

PS: Want to come and see our beautiful venue for yourselves? We'd love to meet you. Click this link to schedule your tour!

By making it a PS, it's not as pushy as making it the main focus of your message. Also, since people scan messages before they read them, the PS is likely to get noticed by being separated from the main body of your message. There! I hope you're breathing a little easier. But, don't stop reading now.

Reason #4:
You Created a Dead End

I mentioned earlier that I have little postcard signs that I give to my sales training and consulting clients that say: *"Ambiguous Next Steps Bring Ambiguous Results."* You may have seen me holding one up on a webinar, or got one in your package when you ordered a book from my shop. It's a very useful phrase. Very often when I'm doing sales training I'll see where you started off your message or sales meeting well, and then it just ends. There's no next step given. There's no specific expectation of what's going to happen next. That's what I mean by "ambiguous next steps." If it's not clear to both you and the person/people you're messaging with, what is supposed to happen next, then you're leaving it to chance. And very often that results in nothing happening - ghosting.

This doesn't mean that you should say: "now you're going to reply to my email/message." You want to be more specific in the wording of your message and the way you end it. This is why in Reason #1 – *You gave them what they think they need*, that they're not replying. They may think that they should read through the information you sent, before replying to you. You're waiting for them to reply. In the meantime, you're getting ghosted, and they're shopping you against some of your competitors, to whom they've also already inquired. The next steps are ambiguous, or there are no next steps at all.

It's also why, in Reason #2 – *You Sent Them Away*, that you want them to reply to your message, but having those links is making them think the next action is to click on them, instead of replying to you. Many of them click the links you sent, get distracted, and never come back to you. It's also ambiguous. Once they click off to your links, there's nothing bringing them back to your message. It's a one-way street going the wrong direction.

I see the same thing on your websites and marketing pieces. Having your contact information is not a call-to-action. Having an email signature is not a call-to-action. Those are just data. If you want someone to contact you, tell them why and make it easy to do so. Don't just tell them to contact you, tell them what benefit there is for them. Let's face it, they care more about themselves than your sale. And I'll keep beating this drum... they're buying the *results* of specifically hiring you (and your team), not your list of products/services. Every other wedding/event pro in your market and category has a similar bullet-point list of services. Sell them what they can't get anywhere else, and that's the results that only you can provide. I'll discuss that more in a later chapter.

So, instead of: *"Contact Us Today"*, caterers can try:

> *"If you want to find out how you can have the beautiful wedding you desire, with food that has your guests raving about it for weeks after, call, text, email or contact us today."*

Or DJs and Bands could try:

"Want to see how much fun you and your guests can have at your wedding? Call, text, email or contact us today!"

Or for ceremony officiants:

"If you'd like to have a personalized ceremony that has your guests wondering if the officiant is part of the family, call/text, email or contact me today!"

In your messaging you want to be sure to include results-based phrasing. While I know that many of you would like to get them to a call or meeting/tour right away, Reason #3 already showed you that it's too soon for many of them.

When you do get the conversation moving forward, and it feels like a better time to ask for the call or meeting, don't just say: *"Would you like to schedule a call?"* or *"Would you like to come in for a tour?"* There's no results-based phrasing there. You didn't tell them why they would be better off if they agree to the call or meeting.

Instead, after you've had a few good back and forth messages, wedding/event planners, designers and decorators could try something like:

"I'm getting really excited about your wedding and already have some creative ideas flowing. I'd love to find out more about your vision as well. Would Tuesday or Thursday be better for you for a quick call?"

Or for caterers:

"Wow, I have so many catering ideas for your wedding I can already taste them. Would during the week or on the weekend be better for you to come in to discuss your delicious wedding menu options?"

Or videographers could say:

"I'm already visualizing your wedding in my head. Would tomorrow at 11am or Wednesday at 7pm be better for you for a short Zoom call so I can show you some of the ideas I have for your wedding video?"

Or invitation companies could say:

Invitations are about the look and the feel, as well as the style and theme. Would it make sense for us to have a Zoom call, or for you to come in and see and touch some samples for yourselves?"

Notice that I don't ask *if* they want to have a call or meeting. We're not doing this on the first reply. We're doing this after a few back and forth messages, so we're developing a relationship and planting the seeds of trust. We're not rushing into asking for the meeting or call/Zoom. This technique of giving them two choices leads to quicker decisions. But again, it's important not to do this on your first reply, as that's why many are ghosting you. Giving them two choices is less ambiguous and leaves the flexibility of them offering another suggestion. If you suggest two specific days and times, i.e. tomorrow at 11am or Wednesday at 7pm, they can always say: *"I can't do 11am tomorrow, can you do 4pm?"* Even if your calendar is empty on those days, suggest two specific times. First, you look busier, and people like busy companies as it implies that you're more popular. Second, you'll get to a decision on date/ time quicker.

By the way, this also works for other decisions, such as deciding where to go to dinner with your significant other and friends. Asking: *"Where do you want to go for dinner?"* leaves open dozens or more possibilities. One evening my wife said to my son and I: *"Pick out a movie on Netflix."* That was it, no more direction than that. Can you guess what happened next? For the next 45 minutes my son and I stared at the TV, scrolling through the Netflix screens, and we still hadn't decided on a movie! In that 45-minutes we could have already watched half of a movie.

The next time my wife said: *"Let's watch a movie,"* I asked: *"On Netflix or Amazon Prime TV?"* We decided on Netflix. Then I said: *"Let's pick either a genre, actor/actress, or something more specific."* We ultimately decided to watch a movie from the 1980's that had won the Best Picture Academy Award, but one we had never seen. That way it was only ten movies to choose from, and really less than that since it had to be one that we had never seen. If you're curious, we watched "Moonstruck", the one where Cher slaps Nicholas Cage and says the famous line: *"Snap out of it!"*.

In the upcoming chapters you'll see more ways that you can be more specific about the next steps. It's not just about asking them to contact you, they already have. It's through your messaging that you can be clearer that they should be replying to you, right now. Remember that you're rarely the only one they've reached out to. You're not only competing for their attention with the other wedding/event pros in your market/category who got their inquiry, you're also competing for their attention with everything else that's going on around them, but more about that later.

NOTES

_____

_____

_____

_____

_____

_____

_____

_____

_____

_____

_____

_____

_____

_____

_____

_____

_____

_____

_____

_____

_____

_____

_____

REASON #5:
YOU DIDN'T ASK
A QUESTION – JUST ONE

As I said earlier, this is my favorite tip from "Why Don't They Call Me?". I truly believe it's the most important tip of that book, and of this one. Along the lines of not being ambiguous, simply ending each message with one question is going to get you more replies. However, that question is NOT going to be asking for the meeting or call on your first reply to an inquiry. Yes, asking a question will get you more replies, but it won't overcome the fact that it's too soon to ask for the call or meeting. Don't worry, those of you that feel you need to have the call or meeting to make the sale will get to ask... just not yet. Remember that Reddit post I referred to earlier? So many of those people were complaining about vendors requiring a phone call or meeting right away. That's why many of you are getting ghosted by good prospects!

I already said that just putting your contact information is not a call-to-action. Asking a question implies that they should answer it. It's as simple as that. Ending your message with a period or exclamation point is ending the conversation. Ending with a question is continuing it. It really is so simple you want to slap your head and go: "Duh!" That's what I did when I heard it from Alan Katz. A light bulb went off for me as I hope it is for you now.

Asking questions is part of normal conversation. If we were meeting for the first time and I said: *"Hi, what's your name?"*, you'd reply with your name. If you don't ask me back: *"And what's your name?"*, the conversation is over. If you do ask my name, and I tell you, and don't ask you another question, the conversation is over. Yes, it really is that simple and obvious. Or, I should say that it's obvious now that you've heard it.

Think about all of the times you've ended a message with one of these statements:

> *"Feel free to let me know if you have any questions."*

Or:

> *"Please let me know we can help you."*

Or:

> *"I look forward to hearing back from you."*

Well, if they were replying, you probably wouldn't be reading this book! All of those are *statements* that end conversations. They've already reached out to you. They want to know more about how you can make their wedding or event great. You just don't know what they want to know, yet. That's where asking them better questions will get you more and better replies. It's also the premise behind "Shut Up and Sell More Weddings & Events." We learn more by listening than by talking. I'm sure many of you heard someone say: *"You have two ears and one mouth because you're supposed to listen more than you talk."* When you're talking, everything you say, you already know. It's only when you're listening that you can learn something new.

The key is to ask them questions that they will answer right away (and not ghost you). Those questions shouldn't feel intrusive or too personal. One time when we were secret-shopping a caterer, their reply to our inquiry for packages and pricing came back with a long list of questions. Besides the fact that it was way more than one question (it was actually 22 questions), the first question was asking for our mailing address. Why would they need that to give us pricing?

Asking for their budget is another question that gets them to ghost you. Couples and customers get frustrated when they ask what they think is a simple question: *"Can you please send pricing info?"* They don't realize that it's not usually a simple answer. And they shouldn't be expected to know. If they've never shopped for your product/service before, how would they know what to ask? Most, if not all of us, are guilty of this when we're novice customers, shopping for things we've never bought before. One of the chapters in my book "Wit, Wisdom and the Business of Weddings" is: *"I'm a hypocrite, are you?"* Even though I write about and teach about this, I've often asked about price when I'm the customer buying something new. Either I already have enough information and just need pricing to see if I want to buy, or I don't know what questions to ask, so I default to the one, common denominator question... price. It's human nature for people to ask about price too soon. In our minds it's an obvious question. But people aren't really only shopping for a price, they're shopping for an experience and the results of choosing you for that product/service.

Another reason you're getting ghosted is that you reply with what I call "high-commitment" questions. These are things they feel are irrelevant, intrusive or require them to think about their answer, or consult with someone else for the answer. One person replying to the Reddit post asked why you need to know her "vision" to give her a price. Another asked why they had to come in for a meeting/tour to get a price. Yet another asked why you need their budget to give them a price. There were literally hundreds of comments in that thread on Reddit, all just variations on that theme of high-commitment questions and actions. For some people, asking their budget makes them feel like the price will vary based upon their budget. Transparency breeds trust. Have you ever been looking for a product or service and couldn't find a price on the company's website? Have you ever gotten frustrated and moved on to a different site? I know I have.

What you want to do is start with questions that they will answer, right away. I call those "low-commitment" questions. These are questions that they don't feel are intrusive and, quite the contrary, they'll think that it's not only perfectly acceptable for you to ask, it's information that they understand you'll need to give them what they asked for: pricing and/or packages. Some of these are to get information that they didn't already give you, and others are to confirm information you already have.

The source of the inquiry will influence how much information you get with the inquiry. If the lead is coming through a contact form, the fields on that form, required and optional, will determine which information you get. As I said earlier, the number of fields on the form, and the questions you ask will also steer some people to not fill out the form at all. You can lose some legitimate prospects by having a contact form that's too long, or one that asks questions that the couples or customers think are too intrusive. If you require a phone number, some people will not fill it out at all, because they don't want you to call them. Of course, most of you will never know that since you didn't get that inquiry. Your website analytics can show you how many people made it to your contact page, and you can compare that to the number of inquiries. It's an imperfect measurement, at best.

I prefer that you don't ask many questions at all on your contact forms. They're already interested in your product/service or they wouldn't have inquired. While the goal for many of you is more inquiries, for some of you it's getting fewer inquiries, as you're already drowning in them and can't keep up. What every one of us wants is better inquiries. In a perfect world we'd all only get inquiries from people who love what we do, have a budget for what we charge and are ready to buy! But, we live in the real world, so read on.

If you do get information such as the date, location and guest count, you can use low-commitment questions to confirm the information.

Try confirming if they've secured their venue, so you know if the date they gave you is definite:

> *"I see that you put Meadows Event Center as the location, great choice, we work there a lot. Have you already reserved your wedding date with them, or are you still working on it?"*

Or confirm the guest count:

> *"I see that you chose 101-150 guests on The Knot form. How many guests are you expecting to attend your wedding?"*

Or confirm their choice of date:

> *"I see that you put October 17ᵗʰ as the date. Were you looking for that date specifically, or are you open to other days around then?"*

Many, if not most contact forms that ask for the wedding date only allow one response. If you're a venue, they don't have a wedding date until they book with you, or someone (unless they needed to reserve their ceremony location first, i.e. house of worship). I've seen contact forms that have a checkbox for: "date is flexible". Some others have multiple fields for: "first choice of date" and "second choice of date", which implies that their first choice may not be available.

Too many wedding venues assume that the date they put on the form is the only date they'll accept, so if you're already booked for that date you respond saying: *"Sorry, we're already booked on that date..."*, which can get them to ghost you. Don't assume, ask. It's the same for many services which come after the venue.

If you're an off-premise caterer or wedding/event planner and they give you a date, ask:

> *"Do you already have a venue reserved, or were you looking for us to help you find the perfect one?"*

It's a great, low-commitment question. They know the answer. They don't have to ask anyone else for help answering it. And either answer is fine for you. If they do have a venue already booked, you can comment on it:

> *"That's a great choice! We love catering there. I hope you're working with Debbie, she's fantastic."*

This is what I call "editorializing" your replies. Compliment them on their choices. Make references to specifics so they know that you really know that business and, if applicable, specific people there:

> *"Great news, not only are we available for your date, the gardens will be in full bloom then and your photos are going to look amazing!"*

With in-person and phone conversations, when one person asks a question, they stop talking and wait for an answer. They don't ask more questions. That's why you need to choose one question to get them to reply, right away. Don't pepper them with lots of questions. They're not likely to answer them all, anyway. Companies that ask three or four questions often complain that only one or two of them get answered. And yes, I understand that this will take longer than if you just ask them all of the things you want to know at once. But this book is about why you're getting ghosted and asking many questions at once is one of those reasons. It's not conversational. This isn't about how busy you are, or how many other inquiries you need to respond to. They don't care, nor should they. They only care about getting their information, and they would like it now! The information they want isn't on your website, and you got them to make an inquiry. Just as when you go fishing, when the fish is on the hook, don't try to reel it in just yet. It takes a little patience and finesse.

Good, low-commitment questions get them to reply more quickly because they feel you need to know the answers in order to give them the information they want. These are questions such as:

> *"Are you having both your ceremony and reception at the same location?"*

They'll realize that their photographer, videographer, ceremony musicians, florist, decorator, and others, will need to know that. If you're a DJ company, and they reply that they're having the ceremony at a location that doesn't already have a sound system and microphones, you can reply with:

> *"That's great. Not only is that a beautiful location, we have the perfect sound system to ensure that all of your guests can hear every word of your wedding vows."*

Photographers, videographers and hair & makeup artists can also ask:

> *"Will you be getting ready at your reception venue, or somewhere else (at home, hotel, etc.)?"*

You can use that to know how long of a day it may be, traveling between locations, where you might want to take photos and videos along the way, etc. Just be sure to comment (editorialize) on their answer, don't just jump to the next question. It's a conversation not an interrogation.

Another low-commitment question is regarding guest count. We, in the industry, understand that in most cases not everyone who is invited will actually attend the wedding or event. The attrition can be anywhere from 5% to over 20%. If a lot of people are out of town, the drop in guest count could be towards the high end. That said, in some cultures the guest count could actually grow on the wedding day. One of my clients does a lot of weddings for Nigerian couples and he is always prepared for more people coming than the final count the couple gave him. All chefs have extra food, but he needs extra tables and chairs, china/silver/glassware and yes, staffing. This isn't just about people wanting seconds on their dinner. This is more people at the event and that affects everything, including the seating setup.

So, if you're the venue or caterer, ask them the guest count and then how many guests are coming from out of town:

"How many guests are you expecting to attend?"

When they answer, reply with:

"That's a nice size for our venue, very comfortable for everyone. How many are coming from out of town?"

Most couples don't want to think about people *not* coming to their wedding. While others might be hoping that some don't come, either for budget reasons or their venue's capacity limitations.

The key here is to make sure you're not only asking a question, you're only asking *one* question at a time. While it does slow the conversation down, the goal of this book is to get you more replies and ghosted less. Remember, the real opportunity is in the inquiries that are ghosting you now. They're going to book someone, and you already made the short list. Slowing it down a little with good, low-commitment questions is very effective in getting you more replies. And don't worry, in a later chapter I'm going to recap how to answer the *"How much do you charge?"* inquiry, using the tips in this book.

NOTES

_____

_____

_____

_____

_____

_____

_____

_____

_____

_____

_____

_____

_____

_____

_____

_____

_____

_____

_____

_____

_____

_____

_____

_____

_____

_____

_____

_____

REASON #6:
YOU BURIED YOUR QUESTION

Now that you know to ask only one question, you need to make sure that it's the last thing in your message. The question itself and the placement are very important. If you've read the recap of the "8 tips for converting wedding & inquiries into sales" earlier in this book, you know that you should try to fit your message on one screen of their smartphone. When we open a new message, we tend to scan it first, not read it through. Long messages get many of us to close them and hope that we get to read them later, when we have more time. Since they're scanning the message, help them see the question by making it a separate paragraph at the end, right before your name. Don't bury the question by writing things after it. That would be the equivalent of asking someone a question on the phone and then you keep talking. You need to give them a chance to answer. But first, you need them to see your question.

I've seen lots of replies by wedding and event pros that ask their question first and then they share one or more paragraphs of information. The question is now buried. When they scan, they won't see it. It's the same if you put your question in the middle of a paragraph, no matter how short that paragraph. Anything written after the question mark is burying it.

By making your question its own paragraph it gets highlighted when they're scanning. So, don't ask your question and then write: *"I look forward to hearing back from you!"* You just buried the question and ended the conversation. After the question, sign off with your name. If you just can't sign off without saying something, make it really short to not distract from your question. Here's an example of the first reply for a venue:

> *"Hi Sam,*
>
> *Thanks for reaching out about having your beautiful wedding at Cross Creek Ranch. I'd love to get you more information.*
>
> *Will you be having both your ceremony and reception here?*
>
> *Thanks,*
>
> *Chris Smith"*

Yes, that's it. You don't need to start volunteering information that they may not need, or that they may have already seen, read, heard and/or watched. Getting ghosted less means getting more replies by making it feel more personal and more conversational. Asking one, low-commitment question and then waiting for an answer is the way real conversations go.

Reason #7:
Life Gets In The Way

At the moment that they make the inquiry, that person is very interested in getting information from you (and probably some others in your market/category). Making the inquiry made it to the top of their priority list at that very moment. They could have inquired yesterday, or tomorrow, but they didn't. They inquired right now. That's why replying quickly is so important. If you can catch them in the frame of mind while they're inquiring, it will still be high on their priority list, or will it? Maybe they had a few minutes to make inquiries, but then they had to get back to work. Or maybe they thought they'd have more time, but something else came up. Or they could get a phone call or text that takes their attention elsewhere. Or their boss could come in and they have to get back to working. Or they could realize that they're late for a meeting or appointment.

There are so many things that can get in the way of replying to you, even if they really do want to continue the conversation. People get sick. People's loved ones get sick. Emergencies and unforeseen events arise. When they click SEND on the contact form or messaging platform, some people know they won't have time to reply to the inquiries, and others don't. "Something came up" isn't necessarily a brush-off, it's very often true. Since so many couples are getting married for the first time, many don't understand that there's an order in which some services need to get booked. I've heard from many of you, who are not venues, that couples reach out to their band, DJ, photographer and others before they have their actual date reserved. They have a "wish" date. So many of them naively think that they'll be able to get any date they want, at any venue they want. But we, in the wedding and events industry, understand that without that signed contract for the venue, or a reservation at their house of worship, there really is no date yet.

No matter how badly they want you to officiate their wedding, plan it, shoot the video, or decorate it, without an actual booked date, you can't say whether you're available. So, what we end up with is a couple who makes inquiries down the timeline and then they ghost you, until they get their venue booked and the actual date confirmed. After the first few conversations with vendors, they realize their mistake. While they could reply to all of you and let you know that they're still working on their venue, many, unfortunately just ghost you.

Life is about priorities. We only get 24 hours each day and we put our time and attention to the things that are highest on our priority lists. While at the moment they inquired, getting information from you was high on the list, it may not stay there for long. Some aren't expecting you to reply right away anyway. When you do, some are not prepared to have a conversation now. You may have done everything right in the timing and the way you're replying and following up, they're just not focusing on your messages now. The good news is that they're probably ghosting everyone who replied, not just you. Well, I don't know if that's good news, but at least you're not getting singled out for ghosting.

Reply every time as if they are focused, right now, on your message, whether it's minutes after their inquiry or later. Don't take too long to respond. A WeddingWire survey once showed that couples chose the first wedding pro to reply about half the time. Speed matters on your end. They may not reply right away, but they will see when you replied and that counts. I'll talk about auto-replies in a later chapter. The short answer is that an auto-reply is not the same as actually replying, with a few exceptions. Suffice it to say that if they're not replying to you, it doesn't mean they're not interested. It could just mean that they aren't replying because, right now, it's just not high enough on their priority list to get their attention and time. And that leads us to the next chapter.

NOTES

REASON #8:
YOU GAVE UP TOO SOON

S ince life gets in the way for all of us, and our priorities shift, it's incumbent upon you, the wedding and event pros, to follow-up with them. It's not one-and-done. Your job isn't done when you reply the first time. You have to follow-up if you don't hear back. Not following up is leaving money on the table. Remember that they inquired with you, and you haven't heard No, which means they probably still need your product/service. When you're the customer and you make an inquiry, and then you get busy with other priorities, wouldn't you like the company to reach back out again? Remember, you made the inquiry, so it's something you want to know more about. So, of course you'd want them to ping you again at a later time which, hopefully, will be a better time for you.

As I'm writing this book, I have someone that I'd like to work with on a new way to market my sales training and consulting. Every time she reaches out, I'm busy with something else. She's waiting for me to do artwork so she can to do a test for me, and I keep putting her off. I could let her company do the artwork, but I'm very particular about my branding. She messaged me on LinkedIn recently and I told her that I really do appreciate her persistence, which is true. Being persistent isn't the same as being aggressive. She alternates between emailing me and messaging on LinkedIn. I want to do it, it's just not high enough on my priorities list now. Good for her for still trying! And yes, eventually I will get to it.

How soon do you give up? Are you replying once and then, if they don't respond you're done? In our secret-shopping, only about half of the companies that reply to us try even a second time (some don't reply at all). Those that do try again often wait too long, a week or more. After the second attempt we rarely see more tries. Some people put us into a 'drip-campaign', sending generic emails at regular intervals (weekly, monthly, etc.). Others add us to their main email list and send messages about open-houses, promotions or other events they're having. I'll talk more about drip-campaigns in a later chapter.

Wedding and event pros who've worked with me, heard me speak about this or read my other books and are following up more times, are getting better conversion. It's no mystery, a business who tries more times is going to get better conversion. Yes, doing better follow-ups certainly helps, but just trying more times is going to give you an advantage. It's like wringing out a wet sponge. The first time you squeeze it, you get a lot of water. But if you keep squeezing, you'll get more water out of it. If you stop squeezing, you get nothing more. Don't be the one to give up. Let your competitors do that (and they will). As I was writing this chapter, I had a call with a client. We were talking about following up and he said that when he's the customer, life often gets in the way. While he might intend to get back to someone who replied to his inquiry, the next call or email could and often does derail those plans. Read the chapter on how and when to follow-up, it's after Reason #9, to see how often and when to follow-up.

Reason #9:
They Booked
Someone Else

Reasons #1 through #8 are all basically self-inflicted reasons why someone isn't replying. Changing the way you reply and follow-up will help reduce the ghosting. That said, no matter how well you reply and follow-up, no matter how good your sales skills, some couples and customers will still book someone else. Whether it was price, availability, the other company replying better or faster, a personal connection (a friend or relative used them), or any number of other reasons, you simply won't win them all.

If you make it easy, some people will tell you that they've booked someone else. Remember, we want to get the Yes or the No. Some people just won't tell you. They'll just keep ghosting you. Some people don't like confrontation. If they tell you they chose someone else, you might ask them why, and they don't want to have to explain it. This might happen if you never got a reply, or even after you've had a conversation or meeting with them. And some don't understand that it's common courtesy to tell you they're not interested. I really can't say much more about this. If they book someone else, and they don't want to tell you, they may still ghost you no matter how many times you follow up. Don't let this stop you from trying. The tips in this book are working for so many wedding and event pros, just like you.

NOTES

_____

_____

_____

_____

_____

_____

_____

_____

_____

_____

_____

_____

_____

_____

_____

_____

_____

_____

_____

_____

_____

_____

_____

_____

_____

_____

What about ghosting after a call or meeting?

Unfortunately, some couples and customers will ghost you after you've had a meeting or call with them. Even if the meeting went well (in your opinion, of course), some will not reply to your messages. Why? Pretty much for the same reasons some people ghost you before you get to this point. Remember the three possible outcomes of an inquiry: 1) They say Yes; 2) They say No; or 3) They just ghost you. The same applies after you've had a call or meeting. If you didn't yet get a Yes or a No, keep trying. Surely, some have booked someone else, and they just don't want to tell you (see Reason #9). It could be fear of confrontation, or lack of courtesy. But surely there are some that just haven't yet made a decision yet. Some of them have had to delay their wedding or event plans, for now (see Reason #7). Others just got ahead of themselves with your category, and will come back to it at a later time.

If you've left them off with clear next steps – as opposed to ambiguous ones – then keep following up. If you arranged a follow up call or meeting with them and they missed it – a 'no-show' – maybe something came up and their attention was pulled in a different direction.

Don't assume the worst, assume the best and reach out again. Try something like this:

> *"Sorry we couldn't connect yesterday. I know how life and wedding (event) planning can sometimes collide. I have some great ideas for your wedding (event). Would today or tomorrow be better for rescheduling?"*

If you didn't leave them off with clear next steps and a timeline, i.e. a call or meeting at a specified day and time, you'll want to start doing that, right away. If you finish a call or meeting and they say: *"We'll let you know"* or *"You've given us so much to think about, we need to process it all"*, those are ambiguous. You don't know when they'll "let you know" and you don't know how long it will take for them to "process it all."

Reply to: *"We'll let you know"* with:

> *"Great, I'm looking forward to making your wedding (event) amazing. When are you looking to make the final decision on your (fill in your service here: photography, transportation, tuxedos...)?"*

If you hear this a lot: *"You've given us so much to think about, we need to process it all"*, that's usually your fault. You're probably talking too much and not listening enough. The delicate balance of a sales call or meeting is to find out the results they want, talk about how you can make those happen, even better than they've imagined, and then ask for the privilege of making those results happen for their wedding or event.

Reply to: *"You've given us so much to think about, we need to process it all"* with:

"Of course you need to think about it. The (entertainment, videographer, planner, officiant, florist...) can make or break your wedding and it's a big decision. If you're like many of our couples, when you take time to process all of this, you'll come up with additional questions you didn't think to me ask today. Let's set a time for a quick call, so I can answer those for you. And then you can let me know when you've made your final decision. Which is better, Tuesday at 7pm or Thursday at 1pm?"

Notice that you're not asking *if* they want to have that call or meeting. You're assuming it, confidently. Getting agreement as to the time and day for the next action, whether a call or meeting, is a good sign. It's actually a buying signal. They're signaling that they are still interested, they're just not ready to commit today. People's buying processes differ. Of course, I'm assuming that you've already asked for the sale, more than once! If you haven't been asking for the sale, then I suggest you read "Shut Up and Sell More Weddings & Events" next. That will help you with your calls, meetings and tours. The original edition is good for all wedding and event pros and there are category-specific editions for DJ/Entertainment/Photo booth and for Caterers & Venues.

The key is to not give up if you don't hear back. I have other little printed signs, that I give to my sales training and mastermind clients, that say: *"If You Don't Ask, The Answer is Always NO!"* Asking for the sale is your responsibility. If you're waiting for your clients and couples to say: *"Yes, sign me up!"*, you're missing out on a lot of sales. That's not normal consumer behavior. Sure, it happens some of the time. Most of the time it's up to you to ask. And just as with getting ghosted on inquiries, getting ghosted after meetings and calls is a part of doing business. It's up to you to follow up. If you haven't gotten the Yes or the No, keep following up. If you still get ghosted, you're no worse off than if you didn't follow up. If you do follow up and get some sales, you're way better off, and profiting more! The opportunity-cost of *not* following up after calls and meetings are the sales you don't make, and the profits you don't get. Remember, it's much easier to close the sale on someone who made an inquiry, and then had a call or meeting with you, who's then been ghosting you, than it is to get a new inquiry.

Use the same 8-tips from the recap in this book from "Why Don't They Call Me?". Be sure to get better at assuming and arranging the next steps. Then, if you're still getting ghosted after multiple attempts, and you may want to try another humorous message, that should get you a few more replies – yeses and noes. Here's one that has worked for a few of my clients:

> *Subject: Did you run off and elope?...*
>
> *Hi Chris,*
>
> *It was great meeting you guys and I thought, for sure, you were going to choose us for your (product/service).*
>
> *Since we've reached out a few times and haven't heard back, I can only imagine that you decided to skip the wedding and go right to the honeymoon, and you're warming your toes on a sandy beach sipping a cool drink with a small, colorful umbrella.*
>
> *If that's not the case, would you still like us to help you have a fun and memorable wedding?*
>
> *Joan*

I love this approach, especially after you've had a call, Zoom or in-person meeting or tour. Yes, sometimes they ghost you after you've had a good conversation, meeting or tour with them. That said, be careful how you word this. While it's working for many of you, a few people have gotten some angry replies from their couple/customer. I haven't seen their exact wording, and I think what I've written above is pretty tame, so I can only imagine that there was something in the way they said it that ticked off their prospects. And if you've already tried 5 or more times, and this doesn't work either, it may just be time to move on.

NOTES

_____

_____

_____

_____

_____

_____

_____

_____

_____

_____

_____

_____

_____

_____

_____

_____

_____

_____

_____

_____

_____

_____

How and when to follow-up

In this chapter I'm going to summarize the 5-step approach to following up from "Why Don't They Call Me?" Some wedding and event pros are trying even more than five times. A couple, who are both officiants, came to a mastermind day I did in Charlotte, North Carolina. They told me afterwards that they're getting some of their best results from the sixth and seventh attempts! I just had Mike Walter, owner of Elite Entertainment, on my podcast (they do over 1,000 events per year in NY and NJ). He said that they have good success with their 4th and 5th attempts to reach out.

While I would like you to keep reaching out until you get an answer, I'd like you to at least try my 5-step approach. It's working for so many of my clients and audience members. If you try this approach, you're likely to get way more answers than with just following up once or twice, or spacing your follow-ups further apart.

Here's my **5-Step approach for following up with inquiries:**

1. **First reply as quickly as you can, using the same method with which they chose to reach out to you** – You gave them the choice of calling, emailing, filling out a contact form, maybe texting or using WhatsApp, social messaging apps (Facebook, Instagram, etc.), live chatting and maybe others. They chose the one of those that was most

convenient for them at that time. Start by replying using that method. You may be able to move them to a phone call, Zoom meeting or in-person meeting or tour, just not right away (see Reason #3 on why you're getting ghosted).

If they gave you their phone number and you want to try calling them, by all means, do it. Be prepared with a very short voice mail message (they may be unavailable when you call, think it's spam or they could be screening their calls) and reply with a digital message right after your voice message. Tell them in your voice message that you're going to send them a message now (email or messaging app) so they'll go check it.

Then, follow the steps outlined in this book and in "Why Don't They Call Me?", such as fitting it on one screen of their phone, ending with one, low-commitment question, etc. I realize that you can't always be the first one to reply, so just reply as quickly as you can, and be the best reply they get. If it's through text, be sure to say who you are, as you probably don't have a text signature the way emails do.

If it's through a messaging app, there isn't usually a subject line. However, if it's through email there is a subject line. Who's sending it and the subject line will help determine how much of a priority they give to opening your message now. Using their name in the subject line can help get their attention. Make your subject line more interesting, compelling or even humorous. Hornblower Cruises, who has boats on which to have weddings, uses the subject line: *"Oh Ship! You're getting married."*

2. **If you don't hear back by the next day, try again** – Yes, I said the next day, not the next week. Put yourself back at the top of their email inbox, text app or messaging inbox. I like to preface it with:

> *"Hi Chris, just making sure my message from yesterday made it through to you (spam filters can be aggressive). I'd love to show you how we can make your wedding amazing..."*

And then complete it with pretty much the same message you first sent. When we do secret shopping for our clients (of their own businesses and their competitors), we find that most businesses try only once, and that's it. The ones that do try a second time wait a week or more to try again. In my opinion, that's throwing profits out the window. Be assertive and tenacious, not aggressive. Be confident, not cocky. Positive attitudes are contagious. People want to do business with positive people, not crabby or non-emotive people, especially for weddings and social occasions. If they don't feel that you're excited about their events, they'll find someone else who is. Trying the next day shows that you're interested.

3. **If you haven't already done so, try a different communication method** – This is especially true if you've been emailing them as your messages could be going to their spam folder. You can keep emailing, but if they're going to spam, it's likely they will continue to go there. So, if you haven't tried calling yet, do so. If you haven't tried texting, try it. If you're messaging through sites like The Knot or WeddingWire, and you have their email address, email them directly instead of messaging through the platform. You might also try to find them on social channels. You

have their names and their status will likely show "engaged". It's a little like stalking them, but in a good way (since they reached out to you!).

4. **Wait a few days (which will probably put you into the next week) and send them one line**:

> Venues can try:
>
> *Are you still looking for a beautiful venue to host your wedding?"*

> Or DJs can try:
>
> *Are you still looking for a fun DJ to make your wedding memorable?"*

> Or ceremony officiants can try:
>
> *Are you still looking for an officiant to help you personalize your wedding vows and ceremony?"*

You can use this approach for any product or service. Just be sure to use emotional, *results-based phrasing*. Don't just ask if they still need a photographer or videographer. Ask

> *"Are you still looking for a photographer (videographer) to capture your beautiful wedding memories?"*

After that line, just sign your name and that's it. You just want to get an answer, Yes or No, so you know whether to continue the conversation. Remember that no answer (ghosting) doesn't mean they've booked someone else. There are many reasons why they may not have yet chosen someone in your category. They might have put all of the planning on hold. This message is just designed to make it easy for them to tell you Yes or No. If it's through email, make sure to use a compelling subject line, not something boring or transactional.

If you're a band or DJ, you might try the subject line:

"Is your dance floor going to be packed?"

If you sell invitations, you might try:

"Will they say WOW to your invitations?"

5. **If you still haven't heard back, wait about a week and try a little humor to break through the clutter in their messages (and life)** - Using a fun subject line and message will get some people to stop ignoring you and at least acknowledge that they know you've been trying. After all, they were the ones to start this conversation with their inquiry. I've spoken and written about this so much that people started sharing their versions of this with me (and some gave me permission to share them with you in my talks, trainings and books). Here are a couple of real examples:

Fun email sent by a venue:

Subject line: microwave or stovetop?

Hi Nikki :-)

I haven't heard back from you yet. So, I figured one of 3 things happened.

1. *You found a different venue that was just so awesome you couldn't resist*

2. *You've been meaning to get back to me, but you've been really busy*

3. *You're binge-watching Netflix shows and you need me to send more popcorn!*

Which number and/or do you prefer microwave or stovetop?

Best,

Amylu

Sent by an entertainment company:

Subject line: Me or Bruno Mars?

Hi Jackie,

I'm following up on my email and since I haven't heard back, I'll ask that you respond with a number that fits the following reasons, so I'll know how to respond:

1. *You're still researching information.*

2. *You've chosen another DJ.*

3. *You've won the lottery and have Bruno Mars playing live at your wedding!*

So, what's is going to be, me or Bruno?

Best Wishes- Tom

Both of these messages got couples who were ghosting them to reply, and both got them sales. Would they have gotten those sales without these? It's hard to say. But since the couples were ghosting them, they were probably ghosting their competitors as well. Most other companies had probably stopped trying by then. Was it that they tried 5 or more times that did it? Again, it's hard to say. Was it the humor? Again, we can't know. All I know is that many, many wedding and event pros have tried this method with good success. My family and I have also received versions of this as customers, so this works for other businesses as well. This one was sent to my son when he was shopping for a mortgage:

Dear Adam,

I've tried to reach you, but I haven't heard back. This tells me one of three things:

- *You're still interested but haven't had the time to get back to me yet.*
- *You've been busy binge-watching your favorite TV show, which requires extreme focus and dedication - I get that. When you're done, we can talk about the show too! No spoilers in the meantime, I promise.*
- *You've already chosen another company for your mortgage. If that's the case, please let me know so I can stop bothering you.*

I can't wait to find out which one it is. Thanks in advance, and I look forward to hearing from you.

Optimistically yours,

Nick
Senior Mortgage Banker

NOTES

Learning to love following up!

Just before writing this chapter, I was speaking about ghosting at a conference. A DJ in the audience messaged a bride who had been ghosting him after she had inquired through the WeddingWire messaging app. The conversation had gone quiet after his initial reply, and he thought he had lost the sale. He also admitted that he was very bad at following up after his initial attempt. While still listening to my presentation, he sent the bride this message:

> *"Have you chosen an amazing venue for your wedding reception?"*

The next day the bride replied with:

> *"Hi there, yes, it's at (venue name). Which is a little past the Paso Robles airport."*

As he was responding to her, she wrote back (before he could even send his reply):

> *"We would love to hire you. What do you need from us to book?"*

After that same presentation, I got an email from someone else in the audience. He had a phone call with a couple and he thought for sure they were going to book him. Here's what he wrote me:

> *"I thought it was close to a done deal since they mentioned on the phone 'we'd be a great fit' and they asked 'how to make payment', but it's been radio-silence ever since the meeting. Just not sure what type of follow-up email to send to see what they decided?"*

I thought about it and suggested this reply:

> *Subject: I know you're busy, but...*
>
> *"Hi, I'm sure you're so busy between everyday life and planning your amazing wedding. Did you have any questions for me, or did you want to move ahead with reserving me for your wedding, so we can start planning all of the fun?"*

The next day he sent me this message:

> *"Thank you for the email example! I sent this message to the couple and got the wedding booked!"*

I also worked with another company on crafting his email replies based upon the principles in this book. I told him to follow-up with people who've been ghosting him, even if it's been a while since his last attempt, as he wants to get the Yes or No, and since most other companies have stopped trying. He wrote me this after giving it a try:

"I also heard back from two couples that were in 'ghosted' status after resending your first response email that you crafted.

One is looking to set up a visit and the other I am in communication with. 👍"

These are just three examples of companies, just like yours, who tried one more time, a different way, and got the sales. And these responses were long after they should have been trying again, had they been following my tips before. Whether you love following up or hate it, whether you dedicate lots of time to it, or little, the investment in replying again, to someone who first reached out to you is worth it. You won't get all of those sales, but you'll get some. And you can be sure that most of the other companies who got that same inquiry, from that same couple or customer, for that same wedding or event... have stopped following up. You could win the sale just by being the only that's still showing interest.

I said this earlier, but it bears repeating; the biggest opportunity for you is the people who are ghosting you now. They already did their research and filtering, and you made the cut. They eliminated most of your competitors, before they even reached out to you. Please don't ignore those leads. It's so much easier to keep trying with these leads than to get someone else to inquire.

NOTES

CAN YOU AUTOMATE YOUR FOLLOW-UPS?

I get asked this very often. On the surface, automation can save you a lot of time. After all, you can write your replies and just program your CRM (Customer Relation Management program) to send them at specified intervals. That would be really easy, *for you*. That's true, but is it as effective as personal replies? I don't think so. There are times when automation is recommended. If you're following up on a list from a wedding or trade show, with people who haven't specifically requested information from you, then automation can help you get to a large number of people, all at once. Some people set up a series of emails (hopefully each adding value and with a clear call-to-action) that go out at set intervals. Those are called "drip campaigns" and they can certainly be automated. However, once they reply to you the automation should stop, and a real person should take over. I once consulted with a wedding pro who used a drip campaign for all of his inquiries, even direct inquiries through his own website. It was very impersonal looking, even though he had obviously spent a lot of time designing the emails and the wording. No doubt it worked some of the time. I'm sure that personal replies would have worked better.

I was once contacted by someone who wanted me to write email templates for their automation software. He would market them as: *"Created by Alan Berg!"* His pitch to me was about all of the money I'd make partnering with him on this. I kept telling him that I don't recommend automation for direct inquiries, but he was very persistent, to the point of being annoying (he crossed the line from assertive to aggressive... and I grew up in New York City and now live in New Jersey, so my bar for someone who's aggressive is pretty high). He kept telling me about the money we'd make on this. What he didn't know is that I won't refer a business, whether there's anything monetary in it for me, or not, if I don't fully believe that it will benefit you, my audiences and clients.

When you're the customer, can you tell if someone is sending you a personal message versus an automated one? Most of the time you can. If you made an inquiry about a product or service and got multiple replies, would you prioritize the more personal ones or the automated ones? I'm always drawn to the personal message. I'd reply faster to an email from a person. When replying to direct inquiries, use your direct email address, rather than something generic such as: info@yourcompany.com. People do business with people, so who them that you're a real person. When you use yourname@yourwebsite.com they'll know three things: 1) your name; 2) your email address; and 3) your website. With Gmail and others, they only know your email address.

Where you can use some technology is by having some common messages already written, ready to use. For example, you probably get a lot of messages that are similar to this one:

> *"We were excited to find you on WeddingWire! We'd love to get more information about your services and any packages you have available."*

Does that look familiar? I'm sure it does. Your initial reply to that will almost always be the same, so you can either copy and paste it, or use technology, as I do. I use Outlook for my email program. I've created different email signatures that have pre-written text, for replies to common messages. You can do this with Gmail and almost any email program (usually the desktop version, mobile versions may only allow one signature choice). The signatures are another way of doing copy/paste, without actually having to copy/paste anything. You create a new email signature that has the text you want to use, plus your actual email signature (the one with your name and contact information). When you want to use it, just choose that email signature from the list of ones you've created. If you're still not clear on this, ask your favorite computer geek (or teenager) for help.

Always personalize your messages after you've pasted them in (or used a customized email signature), to show them that you've seen their details in their message (if you have any). If you don't have anything other than the generic inquiry message above, your initial reply will likely be the same almost every time. Could you automate that reply? Yes and No. If they can give you more details and your automated reply goes out without replying to the details in what they've written, you've just signaled that it's not a real person replying.

A client of mine in the UK had an auto-reply to enquiries through his site, that said something like this:

> *"Thanks for reaching out. We'd love to get you package and pricing info and help make your wedding amazing. Please let me know if email or phone is better for you."*

That was fine much of the time. But one bride had written in her message:

> *"Hi, I'd like to get information about your packages and pricing for our wedding.* ***BTW, email is better for me*** *as I'm at work."*

And then she got an auto-reply from him that asked if email or phone was better. Oops! That's just one example of how automated replies can trip up the conversation.

So, when can you use automation with a direct inquiry? If you've already tried my 5-step method from earlier in this book (or you've maybe tried even more times), then if the wedding or event is still far enough away, you could try creating a drip-campaign to keep you top of mind for when they are ready to choose someone from your category. Just be sure to try to add some value to the relationship with each message. Maybe send planning tips, articles, a photo or review from a recent wedding or event you did at their same venue, etc. Make them mobile-friendly emails, with interesting/fun subject lines, and test them on yours and other types of phone screens, to see what the formatting looks like. Always have *one* call-to-action so it's clear what they should do next and how it benefits them. Write about the *results* of hiring you, not just your products and services.

There is a place for automation that's used well. What I don't recommend is automation that's used to make your life easier, while working against you getting the replies you want. I see way too many people using auto-replies just so they can be the first to reply. Sure, your message gets to them in a few seconds. But if it's not the right message and/or it doesn't add any value to them, being first won't give you the edge you want. Don't send: *"Thanks for your inquiry. We've received your message and someone will get back to you as soon as we're free."* Of course you will, that's expected. If you're not going to be available for an extended time, then an automated Out of Office message is fine, so they won't be expecting you to get back right away.

Something else I've seen, and I'm not a fan of, is an automated message that says: *"Thanks for your message. If you'd like a faster reply, please call us at 123.867.5309".* If they had wanted to talk on the phone, they would have called instead of emailing you. Since you're likely dealing with a lot of digital natives, asking them to call you, after sending a digital message, is adding a lot of friction to the process. And why should calling be faster than email?

My advice is to resist using automation as a crutch or just to make your life easier. Your life will be easier if your business is more profitable. Since it's easier to learn to reply better, and follow-up better, with people who've already inquired, than to get a new inquiry, that's where your biggest opportunity for more sales and profit lies. Don't try to automate your way through this. If you were the customer, you'd want a personal reply, and so do your couples and clients. So, follow-up more and better (and raise your rates if you can), and don't try to automate a personal process too much or too soon.

NOTES

_____

_____

_____

_____

_____

_____

_____

_____

_____

_____

_____

_____

_____

_____

_____

_____

_____

_____

_____

_____

_____

_____

_____

_____

Why do they ask: *"How much do you charge?"*

The short answer is that they don't know what else to ask you. They may have already found information about you on your website, in your social pages, in your ads and marketing, in your reviews and maybe even from word of mouth or personal experience. You just don't know what they know, yet. Whether they've seen/heard/read/watched enough already to want to find out how much you charge, or they're asking it because they don't know how to shop for your service, asking about price is a buying signal. Their first buying signals are out of your view: they get engaged or decide to have a party or event; they go online and start researching, ask their friends/co-workers, etc. Those are all buying signals that you can't see.

By the time you get an inquiry, they already have gone through many steps. You've made it to their short list of possible companies. When they ask how much you charge, it doesn't mean they can't afford your services. Too many companies see this question and assume people are looking for cheap services. You can't make that assumption as it's human nature to ask price when you don't have better questions to ask. We've all asked about price when we're buying things. It didn't mean we couldn't afford it. I've had salespeople assume that I wanted cheaper options when I've asked this question, only for them to be surprised when I wanted to see higher-priced goods/services. *"How much..."* doesn't mean *"I can't afford it".*

If you've heard or read anything that I or others have said about "Top-Down Selling", then you know to listen to what they want, and to present them with products and services that will give them the *results* they want, *regardless* of their budget. You're selling the outcomes, not the products and services. When we're buying things we've never bought before, it's very common to set an unrealistic budget. When we have no prior experience to compare it with, we often start too low. That's why The Knot Newlywed Report said that couples tend to go over their wedding budgets by 30% - 40%. When they realize what it actually costs to get the *results* they want, they often choose to spend more.

I see a lot of conversations on social platforms discussing this topic. Way too often I see people replying that when someone reaches out and asks: *"How much do you charge?"* as their first question, they don't reply at all. Or they simply send their prices and wait for the couple/customer to reply. I'm sure they're losing business from couples who can afford them, because they can feel that they're getting the brush-off or an impersonal reply. I often see those same companies complain that the advertising platforms they're on aren't working. That's a self-inflicted wound. Every inquiry is a good one until truly proven otherwise. I'm sure you've had people reach out looking to spend less than what you charge, only for them to realize that they want *you* to do their wedding or event, so they pay your price.

What if they ask for the price for a: "Basic Package"? A Basic Package for one couple/client isn't the same as a Basic Package for another. Each has different needs and a different definition of "basic". It doesn't necessarily mean the cheapest thing you offer, as that might not have some things that they want/need. If they've never shopped for your product or service before, they might not realize what is and isn't included in your cheapest package. Also, one company's cheapest package may not have things that another company's cheapest package does. When we built our house we went with a builder whose base price was higher, but it included things that other builders charge extra for (crown molding, granite countertops, fireplace, etc.). If we just went by the base price, we would have either missed out on some of those features or had to pay the other builders more for them.

So, when someone asks for a Basic Package, it's your job to find out what "basic" means to them. This is a core sales skill. Don't answer with a price. Answer with questions about what they want and need:

> *"I'd love to give you the price for a Basic Package. Let me first make sure that I don't leave out anything that's important to you. We'll also make sure you don't pay for things you don't need."*

And that's really what a Basic Package is... all the things they want/need and nothing they don't want/need Just be sure to follow that with your first, low-commitment question.

NOTES

LET'S TALK PRICING!

Whether it's asking: *"How much does it cost?"*, or *"How much is a Basic Package?"*, or *"Can you send me pricing and package information?"*, you're going to get questions about price. People can't buy if they don't know how much things cost. Are they asking you too soon? Yes. Do they realize that? No. Remember, this isn't about selling them products and services. It's about having them specifically want the results of you and your company providing those products and services. If it's only about price, the cheaper price will often win. If it's about wanting you, and only you, to do it... they have to pay your price to get your results.

When it comes to talking about price, there are 4 ways to handle the question. While I go deeper into this in "Shut Up and Sell More Weddings & Events" and "Why Don't They Call Me?", this book wouldn't be complete without a discussion of the topic. Following is a condensed version of what you'll find in those books (as well as in many of my presentations and sales trainings).

Here are the 4 ways to discuss price in emails/digital communication, social messaging, on the phone, in-person and even on line at the grocery store!

1. **Tell Them** – if that particular product of service has no variations, or a clear pricing structure, you may choose

to tell them. Just be sure you tell them 'why' they should choose you, not just 'what' you do. They need 'what' you do, or they wouldn't have reached out. Tell them the price, but also tell them why should choose you, and only you, for their wedding or event. Then, ask for the sale. That's right, any time you can give someone the exact price for a product/service, tell them and then ask for the sale.

"It's only $X for (product/service) for your wedding/event. Would you like me to get that reserved for you?"

2. **Don't Tell Them** – If you choose to not tell them, you need to tell them *why* it's to their benefit that you aren't quoting a price, yet. Say something like:

> *"I'd love to give you pricing information, and I want to make sure I don't leave out anything that's important to you, or charge you for things you don't need. Let me get the details so I can give you the right price for your wedding/event."*

And then ask one low-commitment or confirmation question, as referenced earlier in this book. A variation of this is when they ask for a price for a "Basic package," or something like that. In that case you could say:

> *"I'd love to give you pricing for a basic package, I just want to make sure that I don't leave out anything that's important to you, and the success of your holiday party. So, let me ask you a couple of quick questions, and then I can get you pricing for your basic package."*

And then ask them one low-commitment question.

3. **Quote a starting price** – This is my least favorite way to quote price and I really hope that none of you use this. Why? Because the first price they hear is the price they expect to pay. And it's the cheapest thing you offer, so why would you want to only start there? If the price most of your customers pay is not close to that starting price, you're going to be undercutting yourself, and working harder to get them up from that low price. That's called bottom-up selling. I advocate top-down selling, which results in a higher average sale for you, and less resistance from them for the upsells. Some couples/customers also might not think you can do higher-end work, so you might lose the sales you want. When can you use a starting price? If there isn't much variation in the price for the products or services for which they're inquiring, then quoting a starting price is fine. For example, let's say your venue has only one price for renting the facility for the weekend, $5,700. The only variant is if they also want to have Thursday night, it's $1,200 additional, only about 20% more. Most people won't opt for the Thursday, so you could say: *"Our prices start at $5,700"*, that's OK. For many wedding and event pros, the range from your lowest to highest is pretty wide. Many of my event rental company customers have tents that go from $200 to over $8,000. Saying that we have tents starting at $200 would be totally inappropriate, even though technically it's true. If you have products without a big range in price, you could say this:

> *"Thanks for asking. _____ start at only $X (per piece, per person, etc.)."*

For example, if you have photo booths that range from $795 to $995, you could say:

"Thanks for asking. Our fun photo booths start at only $795."

And then ask one, low-commitment question to keep the conversation going.

4. **Quote a price range** – This is my favorite way to quote price, when you don't yet have enough information to give them a more exact price (which is most of the time). To find your price range, just look at the weddings/events you did last year. Put them on a spreadsheet, separate them by type of event if you do more than one kind of event (weddings, corporate, mitzvahs, quinceañera, etc.) and sort each spreadsheet low to high. There's your range. If the lowest isn't a realistic low (maybe it was a friend, very small, or a relative's wedding), you can exclude that. Similarly, you can exclude the highest if it doesn't represent your real top end. Occasionally, many of us get a customer who spends way more than our regular high-end, so you can exclude that one from your quoted range. If your prices have gone up, or you're quoting for a date way into the future, adjust the range accordingly. You can respond with something like this:

    "Thanks for asking. We'd love to pack your dance floor and have your guests saying it was the Best. Wedding. Ever! Our wedding prices range from $X to $XX, depending upon which options you choose."

And then ask one, low-commitment question to keep the conversation going. You may also see a natural grouping within the range, that reflects your most popular price point. You can use that, to say:

"While I need to know a lot more about your needs, I can tell you that our wedding pricing goes from $(low end) to $(top end), with our most popular options starting at $XX."

And then ask one low-commitment question. Or, you could ask:

"Does something within that range fit in your budget?"

For example, I have a venue client whose pricing goes from $104 to $172 per person, depending upon which package you choose. In messages they quote their price as:

"Our wedding packages range from $104 to $172 per person, with our most popular package starting at $134. Does that work for your budget?"

Another client, a DJ says:

"My packages range from $1500 to $ 4000, with the most popular package starting at $ 2500. Does something in there fit with what you were thinking?"

My feeling is that if you are more transparent, and willing to talk about price early, you'll gain their trust more quickly. Too many wedding/event pros try to avoid talking about price. How do you feel when a business isn't forthcoming with price? Have you ever excluded a business from your search because they avoided your price questions, or because they didn't have any pricing information on their website? Don't be afraid to talk about price, you're communicating with buyers!

NOTES

Should you put pricing on your website?

If you're getting a lot of inquiries from people that legitimately don't have a budget close to your range, then it might help you, as it has many of my clients, to have pricing information on your website. Not having any pricing information is going to encourage two negative behaviors: 1) some people will just move on to the next company's website to see if they have pricing information – never giving you a chance (this is almost like getting ghosted before you had a chance!) – or 2) you'll get inquiries from people who see your beautiful photos, read your reviews, maybe watch your videos, and like what you do, only to find out that they can't afford you, wasting both their time and yours.

I've heard from some wedding/event pros that they don't want to put pricing on their websites because they don't want their competitors to know what they charge. That's a terrible reason for not having pricing information. First of all, they already know your pricing. Either they've secret-shopped you, or they saw the prices that you gave a couple/customer who was inquiring with both of you. If you already did the hard work of getting someone to your website, don't lose them by not having any pricing information because you're trying to keep it from a competitor.

If you're not getting a lot of tire-kickers (people who inquire but are way out of your price point), then not having price on your site may not be hurting you. If you're filling your calendar with people you want to do business with, who have a budget for what you do, then there isn't a problem. Keep doing what you've been doing.

On the other hand, if you're either not filling your calendar enough, or you're getting a lot of people who just shouldn't be inquiring because their budgets are nowhere near your price point, then putting some idea of price on your site may help. You can put all of your prices (which I don't recommend) or a price range (which is my preference). Whichever you choose, **putting pricing on your website will do the following**:

- **The number of inquiries will go down**, sometimes dramatically – and that can be scary, at first, especially if you're comparing the number of inquiries to historical numbers.

- **The quality of your inquiries will go up**, as you won't be communicating with as many people who don't have sufficient budgets for your services.

- That means **that you'll have less inquiries to reply and follow-up with**, and that's a good thing.

- **You'll have better conversion**: For many of my clients and readers, that can result in a higher percentage of inquiries getting to the next stage – a phone/Zoom meeting, an in-person appointment or tour, and/or a sale

- Having less leads to follow-up with will give **you more time to follow-up** and that can lead to better conversion and sales, the whole point of this book

One client who asked my help on this put a price range for each of their two venues on their website. They said that their inquiries dropped by half, which as I warned was scary, at first. Their no-shows on tour appointments dropped to zero (people who made appointments and then didn't show up for them). While they were now making fewer appointments, everyone was showing up! Since people already had an idea of price, they were now selling the value and merits of having a wedding at their venue, not trying to justify the price. The couples already had an idea of price before they inquired. Not an exact price, but a narrow enough range, in their case: $19,495 - $29,995. Their conversion rate from initial inquiry to sale went up 3½ times and their conversion from tour to sale went up 10%. So, putting a price range on their site is having a big impact on their bottom line.

I have some clients who put all of their pricing on their website, not something I recommend for everyone. They want to be totally transparent and only get inquiries from people that already know what it costs. If you can fill your calendar that way, it certainly cuts down on the frustration of spending time with people, only to find out that they can't afford your products/services. One venue client has the exact price per person, including tax and service charge, with the minimum guest counts for different days of the week and times of year. It's very easy to figure out how much it's going to cost to get married there. When couples inquire, price is rarely an issue.

Another venue client has the price for up to 100 people for each package, and then the price for each additional person. Service charge is included, just add sales tax. Since many couples are confused by service charges (what it includes, how much it is, do you pay it on the total or only on some parts?), including it adds another layer of transparency for them and their couples. Instead of talking about "revenue minimums" – phrasing that most customers will never use – they simply say:

> *"$XX,XXX is the price for up to 100 guests. Each person over 100 is only $XX".*   (In other words, it's the same price for 55 or 85 guests as it is for 100.)

Transparency can help build trust. Being secretive or avoiding their pricing questions can chase people away from you. You don't have to put your pricing on your website or marketing materials. But if you're getting too many inquiries from non-qualified couples/customers – and remember that them asking about price doesn't make them unqualified – putting at least a price range can help reduce the number of inquiries to a more manageable level.

If you do decide to put pricing, please make it clear and easy to find and understand, not just by you, but by your target audience. I've seen many sites where the pricing was hard to decipher. And others where it was confusing to figure out what was and wasn't included in the pricing. Some have venue fees separate from the per person charge. Some include service charges, some don't. Some say: "Service Charge is additional", without saying how much more. Some include sales tax, some don't. No wonder it's confusing for couples and customers. My feeling is if you're going to put pricing on your site, go all in and make it clear and easy to find and understand. It's a good idea to have someone who's not in your business look at it and see if it's clear to them. If you choose not to put any prices, be sure to say on your site that you'd be happy to give them pricing, and then have clear calls-to-action with links that make it easy to inquire.

Don't sell products and services, sell the results of choosing you

I'm going to end this book with a very important topic. If you're talking about products and services to your couples, social and corporate clients, there's almost always someone who sells them cheaper. If you list what a wedding planner does for their couples, any professional wedding planner can fulfill what's on the list. If your couples/customers can't perceive any difference between what you're selling and the next company in your category, the cheaper price will often win. It's only when they *can* perceive a difference of having *you* provide those products and services, that they have to hire you and they have to pay your price.

The results you provide aren't available anywhere else, at any price. At every opportunity, sell the outcomes. Use emotional and visual expressions to describe what you're going to do for them. Help them "see" that the *results* they want are the ones you're offering. Avoid being transactional in your wording, as that encourages price shopping. Have you ever paid more for something because you "had" to have it, even though there were lower-priced alternatives? It's likely that you have and so will many of your clients.

If all they want is someone to perform a legal wedding ceremony, then the cheapest, licensed officiant will do. If they want someone who will *"help them craft a ceremony that will have everyone wondering if their officiant is part of the family,"* they have to hire *you!*

If all they want is someone to film their wedding, then the cheaper solutions will suffice. If they want to *"watch their wedding video and wonder, scene after scene how you captured those memories, without them even knowing you were there"*... they have to hire *you!*

If all they care about is feeding their guests, then any caterer will do. If they want *"food that delights all of the senses and has their guests raving about it for weeks after the wedding"*... then they have to hire *you!*

Sell the results in every communication with them. Compliment them on their choices. When they tell you their colors or theme, and you've heard that same theme 20 times this month, sound excited for them. If you don't sound excited, someone else will and they'll get the gig.

Avoid listing all of the things you'll do for them and talk about the *results* of those things. Photo booths are *"something fun for their guests to do when they're not on the dance floor"*. Uplighting is *"a great way to extend their colors and theme all the way to the ceiling"*. Invitations are *"the first glimpse, a sneak-peek at the style and theme of the wedding"*. A welcome drink *"sets the scene, right from the moment they arrive, that this is going to be more than just a party, it's going to be an experience!"*

Watch the wording that they use when they describe what they want. Be sure to mirror that wording so they know that you're paying attention and that you understand what they want. If they write that they want a "chill, laid-back affair", don't talk about how you'll make it a "dance party." If they use words like "elegant" or "sophisticated", don't talk about "fun and quirky."

All events, whether a wedding, corporate event, social event, fundraiser, etc. are hosted by people, for people. Ask how they want their guests to feel, what they want them to experience and the main goal of the event, especially if it's a corporate event. Your products and services are a means to those ends. Some people want to know all of the details, and some don't. For the ones that do, tell them, then sell them on having you provide those details. For the ones that don't need the details, sell them on the results of choosing you – and it will likely happen faster, since you don't need to discuss the details.

My goal with this book is to help you convert more of the leads you're already getting to appointments and sales. If you follow these tips, you should get more people responding back to you and you should move more of them to the next step: a phone/Zoom call, an appointment or meeting/tour and on to the sale. Remember that they all don't need to meet with you to buy. What they need is to continue the conversation that their inquiry has started. They already think you might be a good fit, or they wouldn't have reached out. Show them that you're the most responsive, the most interested, the most creative, and the most confident in your market and category. Being assertive is not the same as being aggressive. Following up more times, in better ways, will yield you more sales. It's not a secret, it's a fact. It's working for countless wedding and event pros, just like you, around the world. I hope this book has motivated you to try a few new things. Maybe you've already tried a few tips from this book. Trust the process and please share your stories of success with me.

NOTES

FROM THE AUTHOR

Who is Alan Berg? If I had to answer this in one sentence, I'd say: "I'm a Suburban Renaissance Man". I'm a husband, father, son, brother, friend, speaker, author, podcaster, salesman, marketer, musician, handyman, business consultant, teacher and, I've been told, an all-around nice guy. I'm passionate about my family and my work. I love being creative and working with my hands as well as my mind. That's one of the reasons there's a wrench in my personal logo.

I've worked in sales, marketing and sales management for over 25 years, over 20 in wedding marketing and media. I spent 11 years at The Knot (at the time the largest, busiest wedding media site in the world), most as Vice President of Sales and Vice President of The Knot Market Intelligence. I'm a professional speaker and proud member of the National Speakers Association, the leading organization for professional speakers, where I've been honored to earn my Certified Speaking Professional® (CSP), the highest earned designation for a professional member - which makes me one of only about 800 in the world. I'm also privileged to be, as of this writing, one of only 37 Global Speaking Fellows in the world (through the Global Speakers Federation).

I revel in the success of others and truly believe that your success will lead to more success for me and for everyone. I believe that when you give first you'll get more than you could have ever asked for in return. I also believe in living for today, while planning for tomorrow. I know that this information can help you, as it has for so many others, and I appreciate you picking up my book. I look forward to hearing how you've implemented these ideas.

Thank you.

Please post your thoughts about this book on Amazon at: **www.ReviewMyBooks.net**

Get Alan's other books at **www.ShopAlanBerg.com** and on Audible and Kindle

Have Alan teach these tips to your sales team, association members or group:

In addition to writing books and articles I have the privilege of traveling around the country, and internationally (14 countries and counting), doing sales training for companies like yours, performing keynote addresses and leading workshops. If you'd like to have me train your sales and customer support team, consult with you on how to have a more profitable business, speak for your company, conference, group or association, or have me review your website, please contact me directly:

email: **Alan@AlanBerg.com**
visit: **www.AlanBerg.com**
call/text: **732.422.6362**
international: **+1 732 422 6362**
WhatsApp: **+1.732.289.4842**

ABOUT THE AUTHOR

Alan Berg is fluent in the language of business. He's been in marketing, sales and sales management for over 20 years, working with businesses large and small around the world; businesses like yours, mostly in the wedding and event industry. Before striking out on his own as a business consultant, author, podcaster and professional speaker, he served as Vice President of Sales and The Knot Market Intelligence at The Knot, at the time the leading life stage media company. In additional to his speaking and consulting he also serves as a consultant and Educator for WeddingWire and WeddingPro in the US and Canada; weddingsonline in Ireland, Dubai and India; EasyWeddings in Australia; and Guides for Brides in the UK, doing webinars, live presentations, writing articles and more. Alan is the wedding & event industry's only Certified Speaking Professional®, the highest earned designation for a professional member of the National Speakers Association. And, as of this writing, he's one of only 37 Global Speaking Fellows in the world.

Alan is the host of the Wedding Business Solutions Podcast, with weekly episodes and bonus guest episodes. You can listen on Apple Podcast, Spotify, Google Podcast, iHeartRadio, Pandora and all of the other popular podcast apps. You can also watch the episodes on YouTube and read a transcript of each episode on Alan' website: Podcast.AlanBerg.com

He's able to help new businesses and solopreneurs, as well as established players and corporations, understand and achieve your goals. Alan understands business as he's owned several of his own, including publishing two wedding magazines. He understands what it's like to make payroll, do the books, do collections, apply for a loan, own a franchise and manage/hire/fire/train employees. He knows what you're going through, feels your pain and can help ease it. Increasing sales and profitability are wonderful remedies!

Through his extensive experience, speaking and consulting domestically and internationally (14 countries, on 5 continents, and counting), Alan understands that the needs of wedding and event businesses are not that different from the needs of all businesses. You all want to find, capture and retain customers. If you're reading this book you want actionable content, not exhaustive homework and that's what you'll get. Get started now on your journey to greater success.

Have Alan teach these tips to your sales team, association members or group:

If you'd like to have Alan speak for your company, conference, group or association, do a workshop to thank your key partners for their referrals, get bulk copies of this or any of his books to inspire your team or members - including custom editions with your branding, and to find out about his website review, sales training and consulting services for your business, large or small (yes, even if you're the only employee), contact Alan directly:

email: **Alan@AlanBerg.com**
visit: **www.AlanBerg.com**
call: **732.422.6362**
international: **+1 732 422 6362**
WhatsApp: **+1.732.289.4842**

THE WEDDING
BUSINESS SOLUTIONS PODCAST

If weddings are all or part of your business, then the Wedding Business Solutions podcast is for you. You'll hear ideas to help you sell more, profit more and have more fun doing it from **Alan Berg** who's been called **"The Leading International Speaker and Expert on the Business of Weddings & Events."** Whether it's ideas for closing the sale, improving your website conversion or just plain common-sense ideas for your wedding business, the episodes here, whether monologues or guest dialogues are just the thing to get you motivated to help more couples have great weddings, and more profits for you.

How do you like to get your podcast content? Audio, Video or Written? Good news, you can have all of those choices with the Wedding Business Solutions Podcast.

Just go to **Podcast.AlanBerg.com** or search for us on **Apple Podcast**, **Google Podcast**, **Spotify**, **iHeartRadio**, **Stitcher** and all of the popular audio podcast players, or find us on the **Wedding Business Solutions YouTube Channel** so you can watch the episodes.

Listen on **Apple Podcast: bit.ly/weddingbusinesssolutions**

Watch all episodes on **YouTube:**
www.WeddingBusinessSolutionsPodcast.tv

Full transcripts of every episode, including links mentioned and guest bios are available at **Podcast.AlanBerg.com**

If you have questions about any episodes, or would like to suggest a topic or guest for a future episode, please contact Alan directly:

email: **Alan@WeddingBusinessSolutions.com**
visit: **Podcast.AlanBerg.com**
call: **732.422.6362**
international: **+1 732 422 6362**
WhatsApp: **+1.732.289.4842**

Do these tips really work for wedding & event pros like you?

Here are comments from wedding and event pros, people just like you, who are using these tips successfully:

"Yesterday, a potential bride contacted me via FB messenger and using **Alan's techniques of listening and letting them tell me what they needed we were able to get a contract signed.** I can't wait to use his techniques more."

— Brandon Wofford, *Complete Weddings & Events*

"To me where I find the most value in what Alan has taught me is in the 'why'. **He has taught me how to be a much better salesperson. But he has taught me 'why' it works.**"

— Trip Wheeler, *SB Value*

"I have put all of his principals into practice and boy have I seen an increase in business. **The ROI with Alan is definitely something I don't regret. I only wish I did it sooner** 👍"

— Leslie Rowe, *Coconut Grove Events, Coconut Grove, FL*

"**Alan knows the industry, and he knows sales, and I recommend him to any business in the wedding industry looking to increase bookings.**"

— Stephanie Webber, *A Daydream Wedding*

"Alan evaluated my email responses, website, among other things. **Almost instantly I started implementing what he recommended and got immediate results.**"

— Bob Morgan, *BME Event Group*

"Alan provides common sense, easily executable tips that have gotten me to the point where **I now earn more from my passion than I did from my passion and full-time job combined.**"

— John S, *on Google*

Have Alan teach these tips to your sales team, association members or group:

If you'd like to find out how Alan can help you, and your sales team get ghosted less and convert more inquiries to sales (whether you're a team of 1 or 50) contact Alan directly:

email: **Ghosting@AlanBerg.com**
visit: **www.AlanBerg.com**
call: **732.422.6362**
international: **+1 732 422 6362**
WhatsApp: **+1.732.289.4842**